PERL

MIKE McGRATH

In easy steps is an imprint of Computer Step
Southfield Road . Southam
Warwickshire CV47 0FB . United Kingdom
www.ineasysteps.com

Notice of Liability
Every effort has been made to ensure that this book contains
accurate and current information. However, Computer Step and the
author shall not be liable for any loss or damage suffered by readers
as a result of any information contained herein.

Trademarks
All trademarks are acknowledged as belonging to their respective
companies.

Printed and bound in the United Kingdom

ISBN 1-84078-260-9

Contents

Using arrays

5

Using hashes

6

Subroutines

7

PERL functions

8

Introducing PERL

Welcome to the exciting world of PERL server-side scripting.

This chapter introduces the **P**ractical **E**xtraction and **R**eporting **L**anguage (PERL) and demonstrates how to download and install the free Apache web server and PERL interpreter. These are used to establish a development environment where server-side scripts can be executed. An initial PERL script is introduced to test this environment.

Covers

Chapter One

PERL in this book

This book is an introduction to the **P**ractical **E**nquiry and **R**eporting Language (PERL) for server-side scripting, using examples to demonstrate each step.

PERL can be used to create interactive dynamic websites and is rapidly gaining in popularity because it is a flexible, cross-platform technology that provides amazingly powerful features.

You may have visited some impressive websites where the URL address ends with a file extension of **.cgi** or **.pl**. Typically, these are dynamic web pages served up to the web browser using the power of the PERL scripting language on the server.

The examples given throughout this book detail the source code and the resultant output that appears in the web browser.

What you need to know

PERL code is interspersed between HTML code in the original script document on the server, so it is expected that you are familiar with the **H**yper**T**ext **M**arkup Language (HTML).

Those readers with some experience of other scripting languages, such as JavaScript, will more quickly understand some of the examples but no previous knowledge of scripting is assumed by the book's text. You do not need to be a JavaScript guru to learn PERL.

Required software

The book provides instructions on how to create a PERL development environment where scripts can be executed from a web browser via the Apache web server. This requires Windows users to download the latest versions of the free Apache web server and the free PERL interpreter.

Linux users can simply install the Apache and PERL packages from their distribution CD-ROMs or request their system administrator install them. Alternatively, RPM packages for both Apache and PERL can be downloaded from the internet at websites such as the RPMFind repository at **http://rpmfind.net**.

What is PERL?

The PERL language was originally created in 1986 by a programmer named Larry Wall in order to perform specific data-handling tasks within the company where he worked. Since then PERL has become freely available and has been greatly extended by contributions from around the world.

PERL can be used as a general purpose programming language but is most commonly found on web servers to provide interaction between web browsers via the Internet or an Intranet.

The examples in this book illustrate how PERL scripts can dynamically create web page content and also handle data sent from the web browser when it is received on the server.

This two-way exchange of data is known as the "Common Gateway Interface", or just simply "CGI". Typically, a browser user will be asked to input information into a HTML form on a web page. When the user pushes the "submit" button the input data is transmitted to the CGI on the web server whereon the server can call upon a PERL script to process this data. The script can then dynamically respond to the submission by sending a web page back to the user based upon the data submitted.

PERL scripts are written in plain text and are normally used in that form without compilation into byte code. The PERL scripts are loaded directly onto the web server and are executed by the PERL interpreter which is also located on the web server.

For more on client-side scripting with JavaScript please refer to "JavaScript in easy steps" at www.ineasysteps.com.

This is similar to the way that client-side JavaScripts are run in the major web browsers using the JavaScript interpreter built-in to their software. For instance, when the browser encounters JavaScript code in a web page its JavaScript interpreter is called upon to read the script and execute the instructions that it contain

The Windows operating system does not ship with a PERL interpreter so this will need to be installed before running any PERL scripts on a local system. Additionally, a web server mu installed to create the browser-server environment.

The next few pages describe how to install Apache and PF create a development environment where the example s in this book may be executed.

Installing the Apache web server

Apache is the world's most popular web server which, according to a recent survey, accounts for 56% of all web servers worldwide. It can be freely downloaded from **http://httpd.apache.org** or one of the mirror sites listed there.

Download the latest stable version for Windows. In this example the file is named **apache_2.0.46-win32-x86-no_src.msi** – installation procedures may vary for other versions.

InstMsiW.exe

Note that the Apache installation requires Microsoft Installer (MSI) support to be present on your computer. This is incorporated in all modern versions of Windows. Users of earlier versions that did not ship with MSI support can add it by downloading and executing a free installation file called **Instmsi.exe** from **www.microsoft.com**.

apache_2.0.4
6-win32-x86-n
o_src.msi

With MSI support installed, double-click on the Apache installer to begin installation, then complete the input fields in the **Server Information** dialog box so that it looks like the illustration below:

*Ensure that you name the server "localhost" and that the radio button to run Apache **For All Users, on Port** 90, **as a Service** is checked.*

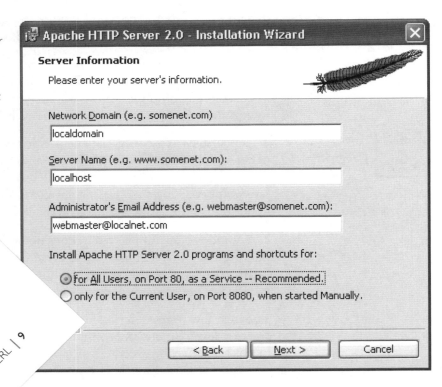

When the **Setup Type** dialog box appears choose the option to have a **Typical** installation. Finally, in the **Destination Folder** dialog change the target location from the default value to just **C:** – this will create the Apache directory structure at **C:\Apache2.**

When the installation completes the Apache web server will be started. It will henceforth constantly run in the background and can be addressed from a web browser by entering **http://localhost** into the URL field. The default Apache front page is shown below:

Controlling Apache

The Apache installation adds an icon to the Windows system tray that can be used to stop and restart the Apache service. It has left-click and right-click context menus, and a double-click opens the Apache Monitor. This displays the status of the Apache service and has buttons that allow the server to be stopped and restarted.

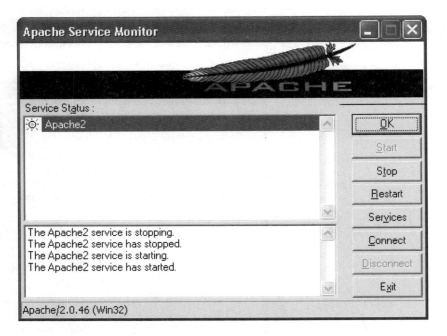

On Windows XP platforms the Apache server can also be controlled from the Services window – to find it, navigate through **Start > Control Panel > Administrative Tools > Services**.

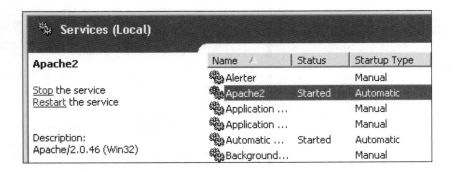

Installing the PERL interpreter

ActivePerl-5.8
.0.806-MSWin
32-x86.msi

The PERL interpreter is available at **www.perl.com** as a free download in versions to suit several operating systems. The binary version for Windows uses the Microsoft Installer (as does Apache) and is named **ActivePerl-5.8.0.806-MSWin32-x86.msi** in this example. The installation procedure for other versions may differ.

Running the PERL installer produces a **Custom Setup** dialog box where installation components and a location can be chosen. Select all components and accept the default target location of **C:\Perl**.

Continue to the **Choose Setup Options** dialog box that allows certain environment options to be specified. Here it is important to check the option to **Add Perl to the PATH environment variable** so that Windows knows where to find the PERL interpreter. Also check the option to **Create Perl file extension association** so that files with a **.pl** extension are recognized as PERL scripts.

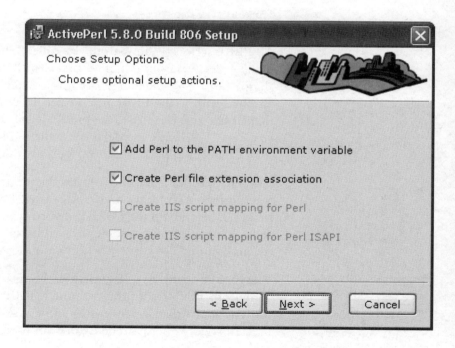

With these two important options checked click on **Next** then **Install** to complete the installation – this will create the PERL directory structure at **C:\Perl**.

Hello World in Windows

Successful installation of both Apache and PERL has created a development environment where your web browser can send requests to PERL scripts on the Apache server. Apache can, in turn, call upon the PERL interpreter to process the code in those scripts then send a reply back to the web browser.

A simple PERL script can now be written to test this development environment. When it is called from a web browser the following script will, in time-honored fashion, output a traditional greeting in the browser window on a Windows system.

hello.pl

```
#!C:\Perl\bin\perl

print "Content-type:text/html\n\n";

print "<html>\n";
print "<h1>Hello World</h1>\n";
print "</html>\n";
```

All PERL scripts begin with the so-called "she-bang" line. This name is derived from the line's first two characters "#" – sh (from sharp) and "!" – bang. These are immediately followed by the absolute path to the PERL interpreter. In Windows, this is a file named **perl.exe** located in the **bin** folder of the **Perl** directory structure. Following the default installation location, the path is then **C:\Perl\bin\perl**. In Linux, typically the path is **/usr/bin/perl**.

The PERL script listed above states the location of the PERL interpreter on Windows in the "she-bang" line. It then has lines that each begin with the PERL keyword "print", end with a semi-colon and contain some text within quotes. In PERL "print" means "output", so content within quotes is output by the script.

*A Multipurpose Internet Mail Extension (MIME) type is a universally recognized resource – for more details refer to **www.w3c.org**.*

The first line outputs a statement defining a MIME type for the content that follows. In this case the MIME type **text/html** lets the browser know that any following content should be parsed as HTML code, rather than be treated simply as plain text.

The "\n" part of the content is a newline character which moves the print head to the beginning of the next line. It is important that the MIME type is defined on its own unique line – so the statement ends with two newline characters for good measure.

The final three lines of code output HTML tags and text formatted by newlines to appear on separate lines in the HTML source code.

Apache is configured to seek files within particular folders of its directory structure – regular HTML documents in its **htdocs** folder and CGI scripts in its **cgi-bin** folder. The script listed above is saved as **hello.pl** in Apache's **cgi-bin** folder ready for execution.

Call the script by entering its location in the URL field of a browser as **http://localhost/cgi-bin/hello.pl** to see the output.

Viewing the source code of this HTML output reveals the neatly formatted HTML tags and the text string – the MIME type is sent as a header only and does not form part of the document.

Remember to change the Windows "she-bang" line when uploading a script to a Linux/Unix web server.

Apache knows that scripts located in its **cgi-bin** directory must be referred to the PERL interpreter because of a setting in its configuration file. This file is named **httpd.conf** and its contents are read by Apache whenever the server gets started. It's a plain text file so can be opened in any text editor for inspection.

The **httpd.conf** configuration file is extensive, but well commented, with explanations. The main setting relating to Apache's **cgi-bin** folder is named **ScriptAlias** and looks like this:

```
ScriptAlias /cgi-bin/ "C:/Apache2/cgi-bin/"
```

If you encounter any difficulty getting the **Hello World** output check each of the steps then check the **ScriptAlias** setting.

Hello World in Linux

Install both Apache and PERL from the CD-ROMs of your Linux distribution or from RPM packages downloaded from the Internet. Some distributions of Linux, such as Mandrake 9.1, install Apache and PERL automatically configured – so that Apache runs as a background service with recognition for PERL CGI scripts. Other distributions of Linux, such as Redhat 9.0, only install Apache and PERL, but require that they be manually configured. In this case Apache can be controlled by typing commands in a shell window:

Remember to change to the root user to issue these commands – the password was entered here but does not print for security reasons.

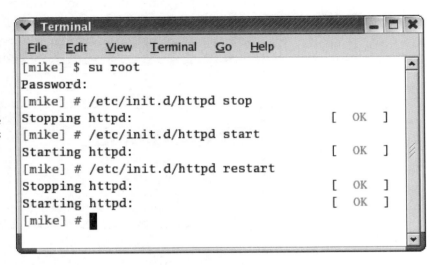

Apache can be made to start automatically by adding the above start command to a boot file, such as **/etc/rc.d/rc.local**. Open this file in a text editor and add **/etc/init.d/http start** at the end of the file. Now, whenever the system boots up the Apache HTTP daemon (httpd) gets started and will constantly run in the background.

The existence and location of PERL can be ascertained like this:

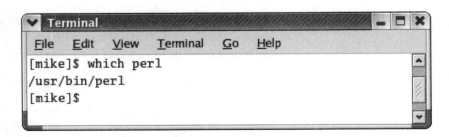

Knowing that PERL is installed at **/usr/bin/perl** Apache can be configured to recognize it. Search for the Apache configuration file **httpd.conf** and open it in a text editor. Find the **AddHandler** directives and, if not already present, add one to associate the **.pl** file extension so that Apache will recognize those files as CGI scripts. The line should look exactly like this:

```
AddHandler cgi-script .pl
```

Now find the **ScriptAlias** directive. This states the directory location where Apache expects to find CGI scripts. Typically this will be **/var/www/cgi-bin**. Save the edited **httpd.conf** file and restart Apache so that it reads the updated configuration.

A simple PERL script can now be written to test this development environment. The following script is similar to that on page 14 but uses the Linux "she-bang" line and efficiently incorporates all the HTML code in a single **print** statement.

hello-world.pl

```
#!/usr/bin/perl

print "Content-type:text/html\n\n";
print "<html><h1>Hello World</h1></html>\n";
```

The script listed above is saved as **hello-world.pl** in Apache's CGI script folder at **/var/www/cgi-bin**. Set the permissions of the script file to 755 so that it is ready for execution.

Call the script by entering its location in a browser's URL field as **http://localhost/cgi-bin/hello-world.pl** to see the output.

Using a specialized editor

Although PERL script files can be created in any plain text editor there are specialized editors available that offer a number of advantages. Most significantly the ability to color code, according to context, and to assist in debugging faulty code.

*More info on **Perl Editor**, and great evaluation downloads, are available from DzSoft at **www.dzsoft.com**.*

Probably the best specialized editor for PERL is **Perl Editor** from DzSoft. This also allows code to be quickly tested by clicking on the **Run** tab, then return to the script code by clicking the **Edit** tab.

It also allows the "she-bang" line to state the typical Linux-style PERL interpreter location when testing on a Windows platform. This means that the "she-bang" line need not be changed before uploading a script to a Linux server from a Windows PC.

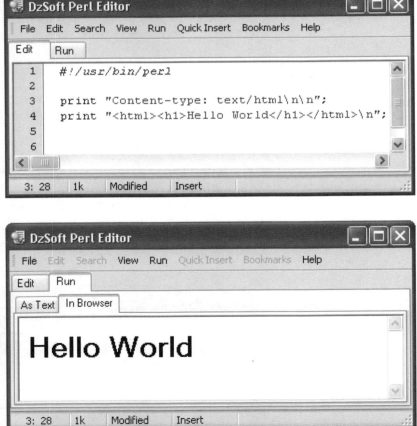

Getting started

This chapter begins by illustrating an alternative way to write the Hello World script from the previous chapter. It then introduces the three types of variables that are used to store information in a PERL script. Syntax rules are also discussed and text joining (concatenation) is demonstrated.

Covers

Chapter Two

Creating a "here document"

The multiple print statements in the previous example can be avoided by using a single "here document" statement.

This is a **print** statement that uses **<<** syntax followed by a label name enclosed in quotes, and the usual terminating semi-colon. Now the **print** statement will treat anything that follows as content to output until it encounters the specified terminating label.

If the EOF is not denoted by a final invisible newline, an error will be created giving the message "Can't find string terminator before EOF" – You must end all PERL scripts by hitting the Return key after typing the last piece of code.

The terminating label must to be on a separate line with no other code and should not have quotes or a terminating semi-colon. Also hit the Return key after typing the final label to add an invisible newline to the file – this denotes the End Of File (EOF) in PERL.

If other code were added to that line, or leading spaces, or if quotes or a semi-colon were added, the label would not be recognized and the script would produce an error. The convention is to use only upper-case characters for labels in code.

In the example below the label is named "**DOC**". The content to output is all the code following the **print** statement up until the label is next met. The content need not be enclosed within quotes using this method nor are terminating semi-colons required – except the one to terminate the **print** statement.

hello-here.pl

```
#!C:\Perl\bin\perl

print << "DOC";
Content-type:text/html\n\n
<html><h1>Hello Here</h1></html>\n
DOC
```

Linux users should change the "she-bang" line to /usr/bin/perl.

Observing syntax rules

A semi-colon must terminate each PERL statement – in the same way that a period is used to terminate each sentence in the English language syntax rules.

Most importantly, PERL is a case-sensitive language where "var", "Var" and "VAR" are treated as three different words.

Spaces, tabs and new lines are collectively known as "whitespace" and are ignored by PERL. This means that code may be formatted and indented to be more human-readable.

A comment line inside a "here document" will be treated as part of the string and will be output.

It is often useful to add comments to PERL code as explanation. The parser sees any text between a "#" character and the end of that line as a single-line comment, which it ignores.

Quotes within containing quotes should be escaped with a preceding backslash to prevent the text string terminating prematurely. Alternatively, single quotes may be used inside containing double quotes as demonstrated in this example:

syntax.pl

```
#!C:\Perl\bin\perl

print "Content-type:text/html\n\n";

#Escaping nested inner quotes...
print "PERL says \"Welcome!\" <hr>";

#Using single quotes...
print "PERL says 'Have Fun!'";

print "</html>";
```

Using scalar variables

A "variable" is simply a container in which a value may be stored for subsequent manipulation within a script.

PERL has three types of variable which each store data in slightly different ways. But all three can store all types of data including integers, floating-point numbers and text strings.

The "scalar" variable is used to store a single item of data.

A scalar is created using a "$" character followed by a given name that may comprise of any alphanumeric character, and optionally the underscore character, but must not begin with a number.

$var, **$Var**, **$VAR** and **$_var123** are all valid variable names.

Avoid case problems by using only lower-case when choosing names in PERL scripts.

When naming variables it is advisable to be consistent in the use of case and also to choose meaningful variable names.

Data is assigned to the scalar using the "=" operator followed by the value to be stored and any text string values must be enclosed within quotes.

For example, **$var = "Hello"** declares a scalar variable named "var" with a string value of "Hello".

The variable can then be used anywhere in the script and its stored value will be substituted when the code runs.

So code to **print "$var"** would actually produce "Hello".

A scalar may also be assigned another scalar by reference.

The reference is actually the memory address at which the assigned variable is stored and is assigned by preceding the second variable name with a backslash.

For instance, **$var2 = \$var1** assigns the address where the value held in **$var1** is stored to the **$var2** variable.

The value contained at the reference address can be addressed in the script as **${$var2}**. This is called "dereferencing".

The example on the facing page shows all these variables in action including reference assignation and dereferencing.

scalar-vars.pl

```
#!C:\Perl\bin\perl

# initialize a float scalar
$float = 1.5;

# initialize an integer scalar
$integer = 200;

# initialize string scalars
$string = "PERL Script";
$var1 = "Hello";

# initialize with the address of $var1
$var2 = \$var1;

# output a here document revealing variable values
print << "DOC";
Content-type:text/html\n\n
<html>
<ul>
<li>Floating number: $float
<li>Integer: $integer
<li>String: $string
<li>Reference: ${$var2}
<li>Reference Address: $var2
</ul>
</html>

DOC
```

The "S" shape in "$" is a reminder of the "S" in scalar to indicate that the variable is a scalar type.

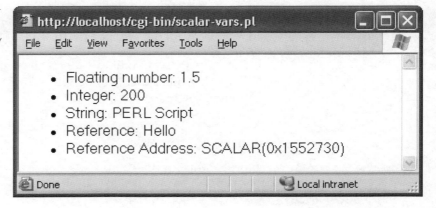

A variable that contains a reference will only produce an address – unless the dereference syntax is used.

Using array variables

The "array" variable is the second of the three types of PERL variable that can be used to store data.

The array variable is used to store multiple items of data.

Data is stored in the array variable as a list of items separated by commas. This is known as a "comma-delimited" list.

Each of the items in the list is called an array "element".

The list of elements is indexed so that each element can be addressed using its array index number.

Array indexing starts at zero so the first element is index number 0, the second element is index number 1, and so on.

An array is created using the "@" character followed by a given name – using the same naming conventions as scalar variable names.

Data can be assigned to the array using the "=" operator followed by a pair of brackets containing the comma-delimited list of data that will form the array elements.

The element list may contain a mixture of integers, floating-point numbers and strings but any text string values must be enclosed within quotes.

See Chapter 5 for much more on arrays and how they are used.

A single element in an array may be addressed using the "$" character followed by the array name then the index number of the required element enclosed within square brackets.

For instance, with an array named **@arr** the first element would be addressed using the syntax **$arr[0]**.

It may initially seem odd to address an array with a "$" but it may help to remember that "@" denotes a multiple list whereas "$" denotes a single item.

Assigning the array to a scalar variable will assign an integer value of the array's length.

The example on the facing page shows arrays in action.

...cont'd

array-vars.pl

The "a" shape in "@" is a reminder of the "A" in array to indicate that the variable is an array type.

```perl
#!C:\Perl\bin\perl

# initialize an array variable
@arr = ("zero", 1, "TWO", 3.142, 4444);

# initialize a scalar variable with the array length
$arrlength = @arr;

# output a here document revealing variable values
print << "DOC";
Content-type:text/html\n\n
<html>
<ul>
<li>List is @arr
<li>Element 0 is $arr[0]
<li>Element 1 is $arr[1]
<li>Element 2 is $arr[2]
<li>Element 3 is $arr[3]
<li>Element 4 is $arr[4]
<li>Length is $arrlength elements
</ul>
</html>

DOC
```

Note that when outputting an array list, such as "print @arr", the commas get replaced by spaces.

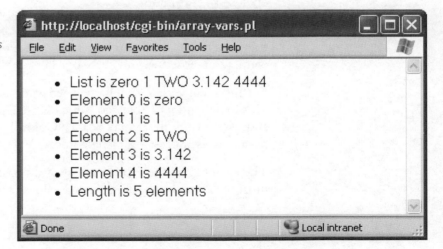

http://localhost/cgi-bin/array-vars.pl

File   Edit   View   Favorites   Tools   Help

- List is zero 1 TWO 3.142 4444
- Element 0 is zero
- Element 1 is 1
- Element 2 is TWO
- Element 3 is 3.142
- Element 4 is 4444
- Length is 5 elements

Done   Local intranet

Using hash variables

The "hash" variable is the third of the three types of PERL variable that can be used to store data.

The hash variable is used to store multiple items of data like the array variable but with one important difference: Data is stored in the hash variable in a comma-delimited list that must have an even number of items.

This list forms an "associative array" that associates the first item with the second item, the third item with the fourth item, and so on. With these pairs the left-hand item is known as the "key" and the associated right-hand item is called the "value".

The value of any pair in a hash can be addressed in script using its associated key.

A hash is created using a "%" charcater followed by a given name using the same naming conventions as scalar variable names.

Data can be assigned to the hash using the "=" operator followed by a pair of brackets containing the comma-delimited list of data that will form the hash pairs.

See Chapter 6 for much more on hashes and how they are used.

The hash pairs list may contain a mixture of integers, floating-point numbers and strings, but any text string values must be enclosed within quotes.

A single value in a hash may be addressed using the "$" character followed by the hash name then the name of the associated key element enclosed within curly brackets.

For instance, with a hash named **%data** containing a pair with a key of "Color" and its associated value of "Red", the value can be addressed using the syntax **$data{"Color"}**. This syntax uses a "$" because it is addressing a single item.

The example on the facing page shows a hash in action and illustrates how keys get associated values from the hash list.

hash-vars.pl

```
#!C:\Perl\bin\perl

# initialize a hash variable
%data = ("int", 100, "flt", 3.142, "str", "Hello",
"Color", "Red", "gem", "Diamond", 100, "One Hundred");

# output a here document revealing variable values
print << "DOC";
Content-type:text/html\n\n
<html>
<ul>
<li>Integer is $data{"int"}
<li>Float is   $data{"flt"}
<li>String is  $data{"str"}
<li>Color is   $data{"Color"}
<li>Gem is     $data{"gem"}
<li>Score is   $data{100}
</ul>
</html>

DOC
```

The pair of "o" shapes in the "%" symbol is a reminder of the pairs in any hash – indicating that variable is a hash type.

Concatenating text

Variable values can be joined together, or "concatenated", in order to assign the concatenated value to another variable.

The "." dot operator is placed between the variables, without any spaces, to concatenate their values. For instance, the statement **$concat=$str1.$str2** assigns the concatenated value of **$str1** and **$str2** to the **$concat** variable.

Also **$concat=$concat.$str1** would concatenate the existing value in the **$concat** variable with the value in **$str1**.

This statement can be better expressed in its shortened form of **$concat.= $str1** as illustrated in the example below:

concat.pl

```
#!C:\Perl\bin\perl

# initialize 3 string scalars
$str1 = "PERL"; $str2 = " in "; $str3 = "easy steps";

# concatenate $str1 and $str2
$concat = $str1.$str2;

# concatenate $concat and $str3
$concat .= $str3;

# output a here document revealing concatenated value
print << "DOC";
Content-type:text/html\n\n
<html>
<h1>$concat</h1>
</html>

DOC
```

Performing operations

This chapter demonstrates, by example, the many ways how PERL operators can manipulate values within scripts.

Covers

Chapter Three

Arithmetic operators

The arithmetical operators commonly used in PERL are listed in the table below, together with the type of operation they perform:

Operator	Operation
+	Addition
-	Subtraction
*	Multiplication
**	Exponential Power
/	Division
%	Modulus
++	Increment
--	Decrement

Mostly the arithmetic operators are straightforward, but some are worthy of further explanation.

Using the power operator ** returns the value of the first operand raised by the power of the second so that 3**2=9.

The modulus operator will divide the first operand by the second operand and return the remainder of the operation. This is useful to determine odd or even numeric values.

Pre-increment operators (before the operand) can be seen in the loop example on page 51.

The increment ++ and decrement -- operators alter the given value by 1. They may be placed before the operand to immediately return the new value. Alternatively, they may be placed after the operand to first return the existing value before finally implementing the change.

Care should be taken to bracket expressions where more than one operator is being used to clarify the operations:

```
a = b * c - d % e / f ;          # This is unclear
a = (b * c) - ((d % e) / f );    # This is clear
```

arithmetic.pl

```
#!/usr/bin/perl

$add = 20 + 30;
$sub = 35.75 - 28.25;
$mul = 8 * 50;
$pow = 2 ** 5;
$mod = 65 % 2;
$inc = 5;
$inc++;
$dec = 5;
$dec--;

print << "DOC";
Content-type:text/html\n\n
<html>
Addition is $add <br>
Subtraction is $sub <br>
Multiplication is $mul <br>
Power is $pow <br>
Modulus is $mod <br>
Increment is $inc <br>
Decrement is $dec <br>
</html>

DOC
```

Windows users should change the she-bang line to #!C:\Perl\bin\perl

Leave no spaces between the characters of the increment, decrement and power operators.

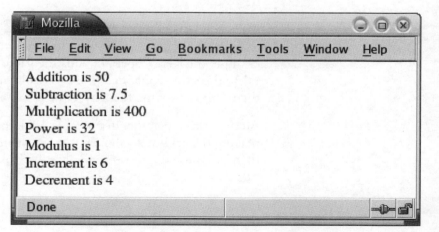

Assignment operators

The operators that are commonly used in PERL to assign values are all listed in the table below. All except the simple assign operator "=" are a shorthand form of a longer expression so each equivalent is also given for clarity.

Operator	Example	Equivalent
=	a = b	a = b
+=	a += b	a = a + b
-=	a -= b	a = a - b
*=	a *= b	a = a * b
/=	a /= b	a = a / b
%=	a %= b	a = a % b

The equality operator compares numeric values – see page 36.

It is important to regard the "=" operator as meaning "assign" rather than "equals" – to avoid confusion with the equality operator "==".

With the example in the table, the variable named "a" is assigned the value that is contained in the variable named "b" to become its new value.

The "+=" operator is most useful and has been used in earlier examples to add a second string to an existing string. In the table example the "+=" operator adds the value contained in variable "a" to the value contained in the variable named "b". It then assigns the result to become the new value contained in variable "a".

All the other operators in the table work in the same way by making the arithmetical operation between the two values first, then assigning the result to the first variable to become its new value.

assignment.pl

```perl
#!/usr/bin/perl

$str = "Assignments with PERL";
$num = 5;
$add = 8; $add += $num;
$sub = 8; $sub -= $num;
$mul = 8; $mul *= $num;
$div = 8; $div /= $num;
$mod = 8; $mod %= $num;

print << "DOC";
Content-type:text/html\n\n
<html>
<b>$str</b>
<ul>
<li>Addition is $add
<li>Subtraction is $sub
<li>Multiplication is $mul
<li>Division is $div
<li>Modulus is $mod
</ul>
</html>

DOC
```

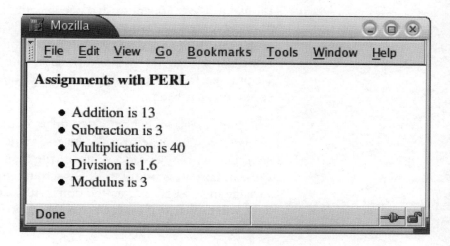

Logical operators

The three logical operators that can be used in PERL are listed in the table below:

Operator	Operation
&&	Logical AND
||	Logical OR
!	Logical NOT

The logical operators are used with operands that have the boolean values of **true** or **false**, or are values that can convert to **true** or **false**.

The logical "&&" operator will evaluate two operands and return **true** only if both operands themselves are **true**. Otherwise the "&&" operator will return **false**.

This is typically used in "conditional branching" where the direction of a PERL script is determined by testing two conditions. If both conditions are satisfied the script will go in a certain direction otherwise the script will take a different direction.

Unlike the "&&" operator that needs both operands to be **true** the "||" operator will evaluate its two operands and return **true** if either one of the operands itself returns **true**. If neither operand returns **true** then "||" will return **false**. This is useful in a PERL script to perform a certain action if either one of two test conditions has been met.

The third logical operator "!" is a unary operator that is used before a single operand. It returns the inverse value of the given operand so if the variable "a" had a value of **true** then "!a" would have a value of **false**. It is useful in PERL scripting to toggle the value of a variable in successive loop iterations with a statement like "a=!a". This will ensure that on each pass the value is changed – like flicking a light switch on and off.

logical.pl

```perl
#!/usr/bin/perl

$a = 0; $b = 1;
$a_inv = !$a;              #NOT
$both1 = ( $a && $a );     #AND
$both2 = ( $a && $b );     #AND
$both3 = ( $b && $b );     #AND
$any1  = ( $a || $a );     #OR
$any2  = ( $a || $b );     #OR
$any3  = ( $b || $b );     #OR

print << "DOC";
Content-type:text/html\n\n
<html>
<table border="1" cellpadding="5" >
<tr><td><b>NOT:</b></td>
    <td>a = $a</td><td>!a = $a_inv</td><td> </td> </tr>
<tr><td><b>AND:</b></td>
    <td>a &amp;&amp; a = $both1</td>
    <td>a &amp;&amp; b = $both2</td>
    <td>b &amp;&amp; b = $both3</td> </tr>
<tr><td><b>OR:</b></td>
    <td>a || a = $any1</td>
    <td>a || b = $any2</td>
    <td>b || b = $any3</td> </tr>
</table>
</html>

DOC
```

Boolean values of true and false can be represented by the numeric values of 0 (false) and 1 (true).

Mozilla							
File	Edit	View	Go	Bookmarks	Tools	Window	Help

NOT:	a = 0	!a = 1	
AND:	a && a = 0	a && b = 0	b && b = 1
OR:	a ‖ a = 0	a ‖ b = 1	b ‖ b = 1

Done

Numeric comparison

The operators that are commonly used in PERL to compare two numerical values are all listed in the table below:

Operator	Comparative Test
==	Equality – both sides are equal
!=	Inequality – both sides are not equal
<=>	Return result of left to right value comparison
>	Greater than – left side is greater than the right
<	Less than – left side is less than the right
>=	Greater than or equal to
<=	Less than or equal to

Equality and inequality operators are useful for testing the state of two variables to determine which direction the script should then branch.

The equality operator "==" compares two operands and will return **true** if both are equal in value.

Conversely the "!=" operator will return **true** if the two tested operands are not equal.

The "<=>" operator returns a value of -1, 0 or 1 depending whether the left side is less than, equal to or greater than the right side.

"Greater than" operators compare two operands and will return **true** if the first is greater in value than the second.

"Less than" operators make the same comparison but return **true** if the first operand is less in value than the second.

Adding the "=" operator after a "greater than" or "less than" operator makes it also return **true** if the two operands are exactly equal in value.

comparison.pl

```perl
#!/usr/bin/perl

$six = 6; $ten = 10;
$is_equal = ($six == $six);
$not_equal = ($six != $ten);
$comp1 = ($six <=> $ten);
$comp2 = ($six <=> $six);
$comp3 = ($ten <=> $six);
$greater = ($ten > $six);
$less = ($six < $ten);

print << "DOC";
Content-type:text/html\n\n
<html>
<ul>
<li>Is Equal = $is_equal
<li>Not Equal = $not_equal
<li>Comparison 1 = $comp1
<li>Comparison 2 = $comp2
<li>Comparison 3 = $comp3
<li>Greater = $greater
<li>Less = $less
</ul>
</html>

DOC
```

The boolean value of true is represented by the number 1 and false is represented by zero.

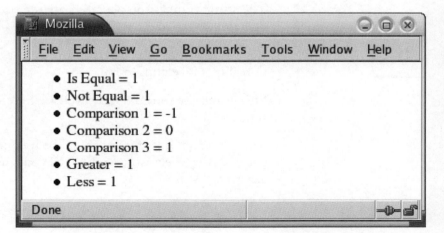

String comparison

The operators that are commonly used in PERL to compare string values are all listed in the table below together with some useful string manipulation features:

The "Greater Than" and "Less Than" operators convert strings to their ASCII values then compare the totals.

Operator	Operation
eq	Equality
ne	Not equal
gt	Greater Than
lt	Less Than
cmp	Returns -1, 0 or 1 depending on comparison
.	Concatenation
x	Repeat
uc(string)	Convert to Upper Case
lc(string)	Convert to Lower Case
chr(number)	Get the character of an ASCII number
ord(character)	Get the ASCII number of a character

See page 28 for more on the concatenation operator.

The string comparison operators are the equivalent of the numeric operators "=="(eq), "!="(ne), ">"(gt), "<"(lt) and "<=>"(cmp).

Repeating strings can be performed with the "x" operator, although in reality it is seldom found.

Strings may be forced to be lowercase for comparison using the lc() function.

The chr() and ord() functions can be used to manipulate individual characters by their associated ASCII code number where, for example, "A" is 65.

string_operators.pl

```perl
#!/usr/bin/perl

$is_equal  = "PERL" eq  "PERL";
$compare   = "PERL" cmp "Perl";
$repeat    = "PERL " x 5;
$uppercase = uc("perl");
$lowercase = lc("PERL");
$number    = ord("P");
$character = chr(80);

print << "DOC";
Content-type:text/html\n\n
<html>
<ul>
<li>Equality = $is_equal
<li>Comparison = $compare
<li>Repetition = $repeat
<li>Uppercase = $uppercase
<li>Lowercase = $lowercase
<li>ASCII number = $number
<li>ASCII character = $character
</ul>
</html>

DOC
```

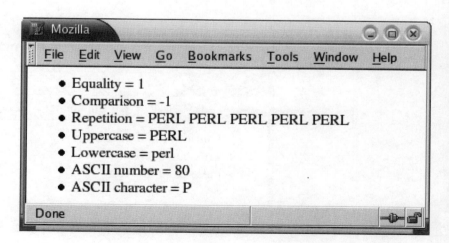

The conditional operator

The PERL coders' favorite comparison operator is probably the conditional operator. This first evaluates an expression for a **true** or **false** value, then executes one of two given statements, depending on the result of the evaluation.

The conditional operator has this syntax:

```
(test-expression)  ?  if-true-do-this  :  if-false-do-this  ;
```

The example below tests the **$is_true** and **$is_false** variables, then executes the appropriate statements:

conditional.pl

```perl
#!/usr/bin/perl

$is_true = 1;
$is_false = 0;
$result1 = ($is_true)  ? "Red" : "Green";
$result2 = ($is_false) ? "Red" : "Green";

print << "DOC";
Content-type:text/html\n\n
<html>
<ul><b>Conditional Operator</b>
<li>True color is $result1
<li>False color is $result2
</ul>
</html>

DOC
```

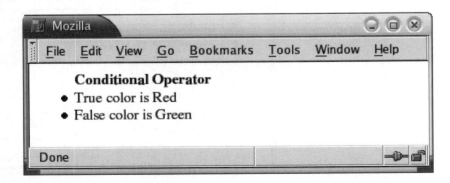

The range operator

The range operator is useful to return a list of values counting in ones from the left operand to the right operand.

It is also useful to define the number of iterations that a loop should make. This example would make 10 iterations:

See page 51 for more examples of looping scripts.

```perl
for(1..10){ print "Perl" }
```

The script below stores the range of all characters in the alphabet in an array variable, then prints it to be displayed:

range.pl

```perl
#!/usr/bin/perl

@lc_alphabet = ("a".."z");
@uc_alphabet = ("A".."Z");
@numbers = (1..10);

print << "DOC";
Content-type:text/html\n\n
<html>
<h2>Range Operator</h2>
<font face="arial narrow">
@lc_alphabet <br> @uc_alphabet <br> @numbers
</font>
</html>

DOC
```

Array variables are just variables that can hold more than one value – see chapter 5 for more on arrays.

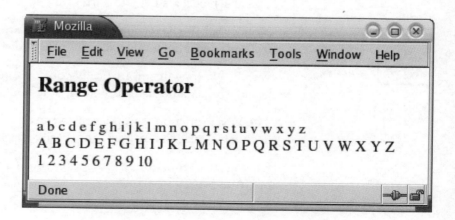

Math functions

PERL has a number of intrinsic functions available for performing mathematical calculations – as listed in this table:

Function	Operation
abs()	Return the absolute value
atan2(y,x)	Return the arctangent of y /x
cos()	Return the cosine
hex()	Return decimal value of a hexidecimal string
oct()	Return decimal value of an octal string
sin()	Return the sine
sqrt()	Return the square root

All these functions will perform a mathematical calculation on a value placed inside the brackets after the function name.

Atan2() returns the angle, in radians, from the X axis to a point at the position (y,x) in the range -PI to PI.

The value will be negative if y is negative and positive if y is positive. The result will be zero if y is zero.

The **abs()**, **cos()**, **sin()** and **sqrt()** functions all act as expected.

The hex() function is used in the form parser code on page 128.

Notice that the **hex()** and **oct()** functions are used to convert values from hexadecimal and octal, rather than into those formats.

Web browsers will automatically convert some data into hexadecimal values before sending it to a CGI script.

The **hex()** function is important to convert that data back into decimal format so it can be more easily handled in the script.

Each of these functions are demonstrated by the examples on the opposite page.

math.pl

```perl
#!/usr/bin/perl

$absolute = abs(-100);
$arc = atan2(100,200);
$cosine = cos(100);
$from_hex = hex(10);
$from_oct = oct(10);
$sine = sin(100);
$sq_root = sqrt(144);

print << "DOC";
Content-type:text/html\n\n
<html>
<ul>
<li>Absolute is $absolute
<li>Arc is $arc
<li>Cosine is $cosine
<li>From hexadecimal is $from_hex
<li>From octal is $from_oct
<li>Sine is $sine
<li>Square root is $sq_root
</ul>
</html>

DOC
```

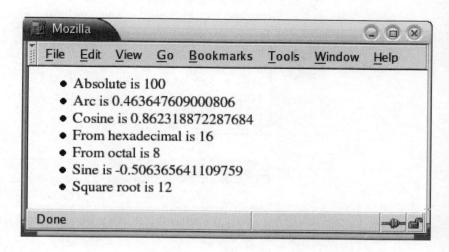

Escape sequences

When a character in a string is preceded by the backslash character "\" there is a special effect on the character immediately following the backslash. This is known as an escape sequence as it allows the character to escape recognition as part of the PERL syntax. The table below lists common escape sequences:

\n	New line
\l	Lower case next character
\u	Upper case next character
\L	Lower case until \E is found
\U	Upper case until \E is found
\'	Single quote that will not terminate a string
\"	Double quote that will not terminate a string
\\	Single backslash character

Paired single quotes may be nested inside double quotes without the backslash escape character.

The escape sequence " \" " is useful to incorporate quotation marks within a string without the string being terminated.

Several escape sequences are used in the code below to format the text and to add nested quotes without terminating the string:

escape.pl

```
#!/usr/bin/perl

$ln1 = "We say \"PERL is cool\"";
$ln2 = " \\ \ulet\'s have \Umore.\E";

print "Content-type:text/html\n\n<html>$ln1$ln2</html>";
```

Making statements

This chapter shows, by example, how to write statements in PERL scripts. Conditional branching is demonstrated and each type of loop statement is explained and illustrated.

Covers

Chapter Four

Conditional if

A statement is simply any valid PERL code that will perform some action within a script.

The "if" keyword is used to perform the basic conditional PERL test to evaluate an expression for a boolean value.

The statement following the evaluation will only be executed when the expression returns **true**.

The syntax for the "if" statement looks like this:

```
if( test-expression ) { statement-to-execute-if-true }
```

Curly brackets are also known as "braces".

Notice that the test expression is enclosed in standard brackets and the statement to execute is enclosed in curly brackets.

The example below contains two conditional tests – but only the statement following the test returning **true** is executed:

if.pl

```perl
#!C:\Perl\bin\perl

$sky = "blue";

print "Content-type:text/html\n\n";
print "<html><h2>The weather is ";

if ($sky eq "gray") { print "cloudy" };
if ($sky eq "blue") { print "sunny" };

print "</h2></html>";
```

Multiple statements

The curly brackets that follow a conditional test may contain more than one statement.

When the test returns **true** all statements that are enclosed within the curly brackets after the test will be executed.

The code within the curly brackets that makes multiple statements is known as the "statement block".

The following example builds on the previous example to add multiple statements to be executed after a **true** test:

statement-block.pl

```
#!C:\Perl\bin\perl

$sky = "blue";

if( $sky eq "blue" )
{ $weather = "sunny"; $mood = "happy"; }

if( $sky eq "gray" )
{ $weather = "cloudy"; $mood = "gloomy"; }

print << "DOC";
Content-type:text/html\n\n
<html><h2>
Today the weather is $weather <br>
and everyone is $mood.
</h2></html>

DOC
```

The final "else" statement in this block is used to set default values in the event that none of the preceding tests return true.

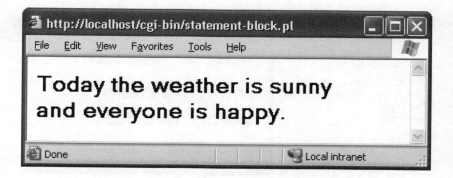

Else alternative

The PERL keyword "else" is used with an "if" conditional test to provide alternative code that will be executed when the test returns **false**.

This arrangement determines the direction that the script will take and is known as "conditional branching".

In the following example the script tests two numbers to determine if they are odd or even then writes the appropriate result in the HTML code:

else.pl

```
#!C:\Perl\bin\perl

$num1 = 10;
$num2 = 11;

print "Content-type:text/html\n\n";
print "<html><h2>";

if( $num1 % 2 == 0 )
{ print "\$num1 is even. <br>" }
else
{ print "\$num1 is odd. <br>" }

if( $num2 % 2 == 0 )
{ print "\$num2 is even." }
else
{ print "\$num2 is odd." }

print "</h2></html>";
```

Remember to escape the "$" character with a backslash to use it literally.

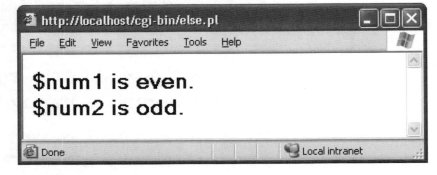

Elsif alternative

An "if" block may test multiple alternatives with the "elsif" PERL keyword. This combines an "else" alternative with a new "if" conditional test.

The script will test each condition until a test returns **true**.

Statements associated with that test will then be executed and no more code is parsed in that "if" block.

This is demonstrated in the example below which returns **true** at the first "elsif" conditional test. Its associated **$shade** variable is assigned the string value of "navy", then parsing ends in this "if" block.

elsif.pl

```
#!C:\Perl\bin\perl

$hue = "blue";

if( $hue eq "red" ) { $shade = "crimson" }
elsif( $hue eq "blue" ) { $shade = "navy" }
elsif( $hue eq "blue" ) { $shade = "royal" }
else { $hue = "yellow"; $shade = "lemon" };

print << "DOC";
Content-type:text/html\n\n
<html><h1>
Shade is $shade
</h2></html>

DOC
```

*The final "else" statement in this block is used to set default values in the event that none of the preceding tests return **true**.*

The spelling of "elsif" has only a single "e" and is not "elseif".

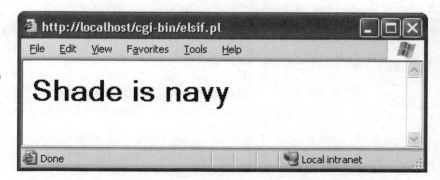

For loop

The "for" loop is probably the most frequently used type of loop that is found in PERL scripts and has this syntax:

```
for(initializer, test, increment/decrement) {statements}
```

The code contained in the statement block will be executed at each "pass", or "iteration" of the loop.

The initializer is used to set the starting value of a counter that keeps track of the number of loop iterations.

A variable is declared to act as the counter and is assigned a value that is the starting point of the loop.

Traditionally the variable used as the counter is named **$i**.

To start a loop counting from zero the initializer would be declared with **$i=0**.

At each iteration of the loop a conditional test is made and the loop will only continue if the test returns **true**.

If the test returns **false** then the loop will end.

The conditional test commonly specifies an end point for the loop by setting an extreme limit for the counter value.

When counting up, the "less than" operator "<" will return **true** until the counter's upper limit is reached.

When counting down the "greater than" operator ">" will return **true** until the counter's lower limit is reached.

Because the loop starts at zero, not one, the limit is the same number as the number of iterations.

To loop ten times in an incrementing loop starting at zero the conditional test would be declared with **$i<10**.

With every iteration of a "for" loop the value of the counter variable is incremented, or decremented. If the conditional test still returns **true** the statement block is then executed.

The example on the facing page makes ten iterations and changes the assigned value of two variables at each pass.

...cont'd

for.pl

```
#!C:\Perl\bin\perl

$up = 0;
$dn = 0;

print "Content-type:text/html\n\n";
print "<html><ul>";

for( $i=0; $i<10; $i++ )
{
    ++$up;
    --$dn;
    print "<li>Rising is $up ";
    print "Falling is $dn";
}

print "</ul></html>";
```

Placing the increment or decrement operators before an operand immediately returns its new value. Change ++$up to $up++ to see the difference.

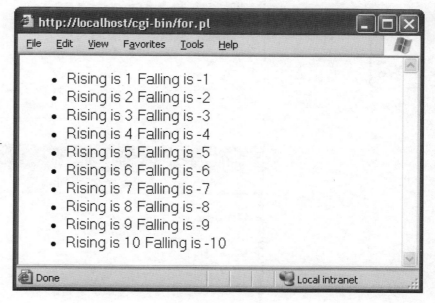

Conditional unless

Another conditional test can be made using the "unless" PERL keyword to preclude the execution of a statement when the test returns **true**.

An "if" conditional test could be used for this purpose but the code is simpler and more elegant using "unless" instead.

The example below would normally print a list from 1 to 9 but the "unless" statement precludes all the even numbers:

unless.pl

```
#!C:/Perl/bin/perl

print "Content-type:text/html\n\n";

print "<html><h4>Unless</h4><ul>";

for( $i=1; $i<10; $i++ )
{
  unless( $i % 2 == 0 )
  {
    print "<li>\$i is $i";
  }
}

print "</ul></html>";
```

In this example the equivalent conditional test can be made using this code:

if (($i % 2 == 0) ==0)

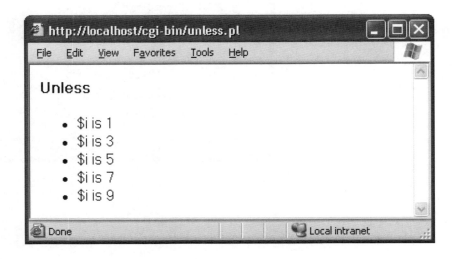

Until loop

The PERL "until" keyword can be used to make a simple loop.

An "until" loop performs a conditional test then, if the test returns **false**, will execute the code in its statement block.

This continues until the test returns **true** and the loop ends.

In this example the print statement is executed and the variable is incremented on each iteration. When the variable value reaches 6 the test returns **true** and the loop ends.

until.pl

There must always be an expression in the statement block that changes the tested value. Otherwise the loop becomes an "infinite loop" that will never end.

```perl
#!C:\Perl\bin\perl

print "Content-type:text/html\n\n";

print "<html><h4>Until Loop</h4><ul>";

$count = 1;

until( $count == 6 )
{
    print "<li>Count is $count";
    $count++;
}

print "</ul></html>";
```

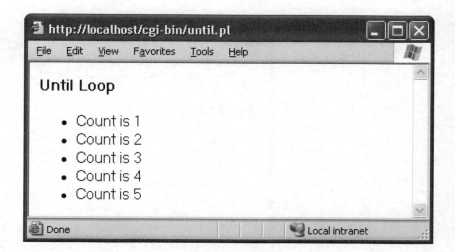

http://localhost/cgi-bin/until.pl

File   Edit   View   Favorites   Tools   Help

Until Loop

- Count is 1
- Count is 2
- Count is 3
- Count is 4
- Count is 5

Done   Local intranet

While loop

The PERL "while" keyword can be used to make a loop similar to an "until" loop – but with one major difference.

With "until" the loop continues until the test returns **true** whereas a "while" loop continues until the test returns **false**.

A "while" loop performs a conditional test then, if the test returns **true**, will execute the code in its statement block.

In this example the print statement is executed and the variable is incremented on each iteration. When the variable value reaches 6 the test returns **false** and the loop ends.

while.pl

```
#!C:\Perl\bin\perl

print "Content-type:text/html\n\n";
print "<html><h4>While Loop</h4><ul>";

$count = 1;

while( $count < 6 )
{
    print "<li>Count is $count";
    $count++;
}

print "</ul></html>";
```

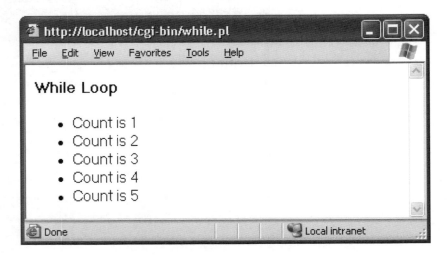

Do loop

A "do" loop is unusual in having its conditional test after the statement block. This means that the statements contained in a "do" loop will always run at least once.

The "do" loop can use either a "while" statement or an "until" statement as its conditional test.

In the example below a "while" statement tests the **$count** variable value and ends the loop when this value reaches 6.

do.pl

```
#!C:\Perl\bin\perl

print "Content-type:text/html\n\n";
print "<html><h4>Do Loop</h4><ul>";

$count = 1;

do
{
    print "<li>Count is $count";
    $count++;
}
while($count<6);

print "</ul></html>";
```

Because "while" statements are commonly used to test in "do" loops this loop is also known as "do-while".

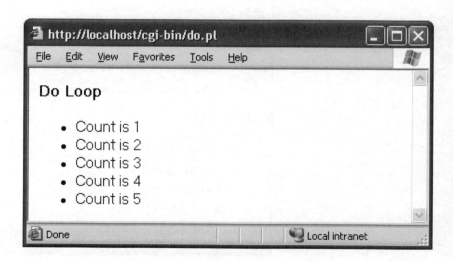

http://localhost/cgi-bin/do.pl

File   Edit   View   Favorites   Tools   Help

Do Loop

- Count is 1
- Count is 2
- Count is 3
- Count is 4
- Count is 5

Done   Local intranet

Next jump

The PERL "next" keyword is used to stop the current iteration of any loop, and then continue with the loop's next iteration.

It is useful to prevent the execution of statements for an iteration when a certain test condition is met.

For example, the script below illustrates a "for" loop that would normally write a HTML line at every pass.

The "next" statement prevents the execution of the print statement for the iteration when the tested value is 3.

However, the loop does continue with the next iteration.

next.pl

The "next", "last" & "redo" statements all jump to a previous point in the script – so they are known as "jump statements".

```perl
#!C:\Perl\bin\perl

print "Content-type:text/html\n\n";
print "<html><h4>Next Jump</h4><ul>";

for( $i=1; $i<6; $i++ )
{
    if( $i == 3 ){ next }

    print "<li>Count is is $i";
}

print "</ul></html>";
```

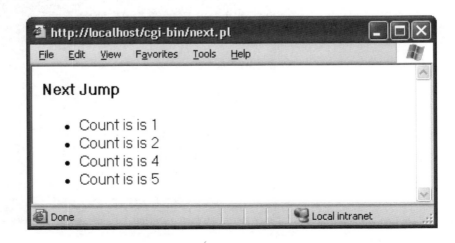

Last jump

The "last" PERL keyword is used to stop the current iteration of any loop and exit the loop without any further passes.

This is useful to terminate a loop instantly when a certain test condition has been met.

For example, the script below illustrates a "while" loop that would normally write a HTML line at every pass.

The "last" statement prevents the execution of the print statement for the iteration when the tested value is 4.

The loop ends and does not continue with the next iteration.

last.pl

The "last" statement must come before other statements in the statement block to avoid them being executed.

```
#!C:\Perl\bin\perl

print "Content-type:text/html\n\n";
print "<html><h4>Last Jump</h4><ul>";

$count=1;

while( $count < 6 )
{
    if( $count == 4 ) { last }

    print "<li>Count is $count";
    $count++;
}

print "</ul></html>";
```

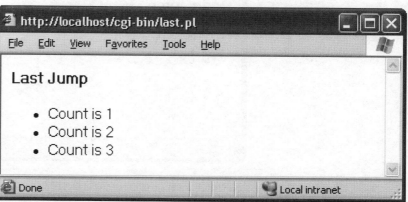

Redo jump

The "redo" PERL keyword can be placed at the end of a statement block to repeat its execution.

This creates a loop by iterating the statements code repeatedly. It is important to create a means of exit in order to avoid creating an infinite loop.

The example below uses a "last" statement as a way to exit.

redo.pl

A loop of this kind is seldom found in reality. It is included here to illustrate the adage that "PERL always provides more than one way to do anything".

```perl
#!C:\Perl\bin\perl

print "Content-type:text/html\n\n";
print "<html><h4>Redo Jump</h4><ul>";

$count = 1;

{
    if( $count > 5 ) { last }

    print "<li>Count is $count";
    $count++;
    redo;
}

print "</ul></html>";
```

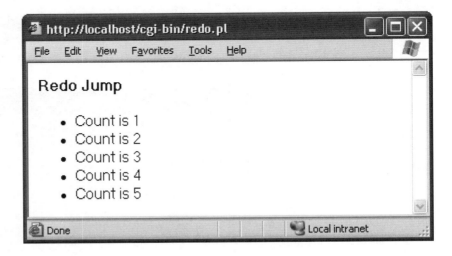

Using arrays

This chapter is devoted to the array variable. Unlike the scalar variable, which holds a single value, an array can contain multiple values. The examples in this chapter demonstrate how to manipulate the data stored in array variables.

Covers

Chapter Five

Creating an array

An array is declared in PERL with the "@" character, followed by a given name. The designated name should use the same naming conventions that apply when naming scalar variables.

Naming rules for variables are discussed on page 22.

A list of data items can then be assigned to the array variable using the "=" character followed by the list within brackets.

The items in the list must be separated by commas and string items must be enclosed within quotes.

Because the assignation of single word lists is common, PERL has a special inbuilt function "qw()" that permits the words to be listed without quotes and separated only by a space.

This example declares three arrays and assigns lists to them:

arrays.pl

```perl
#!/usr/bin/perl

@words1 = ("dog","cat","bird","fish");
@words2 = qw(dog cat bird fish);
@numbrs = (1,2,3,4.567);

print << "DOC";
Content-type:text/html\n\n
<html><ul>
<li>@words1
<li>@words2
<li>@numbrs
</ul></html>

DOC
```

The "@" symbol is a reminder of the "A" in "Array".

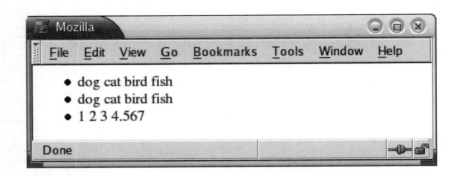

Referencing elements

The list of items stored in an array are referred to as "elements" and are numerically indexed starting at zero.

Each element can be referenced using its index number contained within square brackets after the array name.

The array name must be preceded by the "$" character when addressing single pieces of data, not the "@" array symbol.

Assigning an array to a scalar assigns the total array length.

Elements can also be addressed backwards from the last element starting at -1, as illustrated in this example:

elements.pl

The first element in an array is index number zero – not index number one.

```perl
#!/usr/bin/perl

@words = ("dog","cat","bird","fish");

$words_length = @words;

print << "DOC";
Content-type:text/html\n\n
<html><ul>
<li>First element is $words[0]
<li>Final element is $words[-1]
<li>Array length is $words_length
</ul></html>

DOC
```

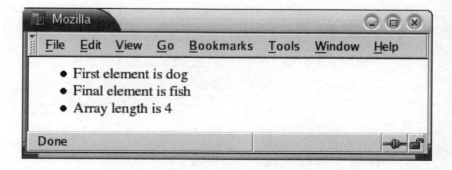

Converting scalars to arrays

The intrinsic PERL function "split()" can be used to fill the elements of an array from a **$scalar** value.

This function requires two arguments to specify the scalar name and at what points the scalar value should be split.

If the scalar value is a text string with single spaces between the words then the string can be split by specifying the space as the points at which to split the scalar.

If the value is a list separated by commas, then the comma can be specified as the point at which to split. Specify the point between two forward-slash characters when defining the argument as seen in this example:

split.pl

```perl
#!/usr/bin/perl

$str = "PERL in easy steps";
@words = split( / / ,$str );

$numlist = "1,2,3,4,5";
@nums = split( /,/ ,$numlist);

print << "DOC";
Content-type:text/html\n\n
<html><ul>
<li>@words
<li>$words[2]
<li>@nums
</ul></html>

DOC
```

Notice that the output will automatically supply a space between the element values.

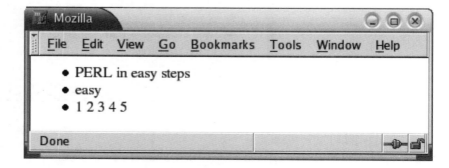

A fill-elements loop

A loop can be used to efficiently fill the elements of an array by assigning a value to each element in turn.

The first loop iteration can address the first array element and assign a value to it. On the next iteration the second element can be assigned a value. This process continues until all the data has been stored inside array elements.

In the example below a "for" loop runs 5 iterations.

Each iteration assigns a concatenated string value to successive elements then writes them into a HTML list.

fill.pl

HOT TIP

The array will expand in size to have the number of elements that is required for the data.

```perl
#!/usr/bin/perl

print "Content-type:text/html\n\n";
print "<html><ul>";

for( $i=0; $i<5; $i++ )
{
    $arr[$i]="Element Number ".$i;
    print "<li>$arr[$i]";
}

print "</ul></html>";
```

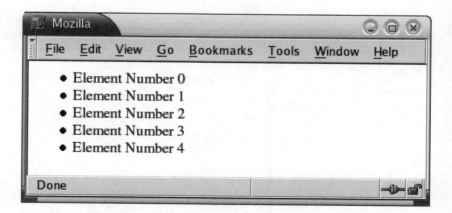

Addressing all elements

The "foreach" PERL keyword is used to create a special kind of loop that will list each element value in an array variable.

Each element value is assigned to a single scalar variable in succession on each iteration of the loop.

The current value contained by the scalar variable can be used within the loop's statement block to process that element's data.

In the example below each element value is assigned to a variable named **$pet** then written into a HTML list:

foreach.pl

```perl
#!/usr/bin/perl

@pets = ("dog", "cat", "bird", "fish");

print "Content-type:text/html\n\n";
print "<html><ul><h4>Foreach Loop</h4>";

foreach $pet (@pets){
print "<li>$pet";
}

print "</ul></html>";
```

The way that the curly brackets are positioned in this example is the recognized normal format. Examples given in this book may also use other formats in order to clarify code.

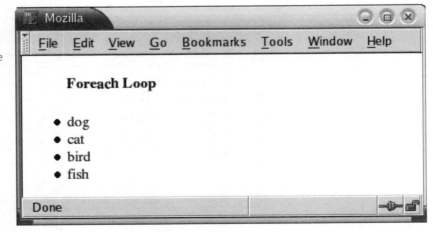

Subarrays

A subarray is an array whose element values have been assigned from selected elements of another array.

Multiple selected elements of an array can be addressed using the square brackets that follow the array name.

The "$" character is only used to address single items of data.

The index numbers must be separated by a comma. Also the array name should be preceded by the "@" symbol because it addresses multiple items of data.

The example below creates an array of weekday names then assigns selected ones to a subarray.

The HTML output displays the weekday names array, the subarray and a further multiple selection:

subarray.pl

```perl
#!/usr/bin/perl

@arr = ("mon","tue","wed","thu","fri");
@subarray = @arr[0,2,4];

print << "DOC";
Content-type:text/html\n\n
<html><ul>
<li>Array is :@arr
<li>Subarray is :@subarray
<li>Selected elements are :@arr[1,3];
</ul></html>

DOC
```

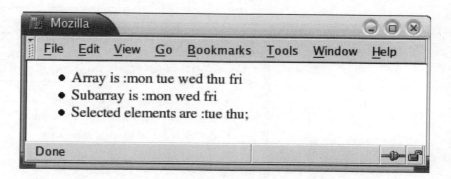

Addressing from the end of the array, the subarray could be assigned the same selected elements with @subarray=@arr[-5,-3,-1];

Add/remove first element

The PERL "unshift()" function is used to add new elements at the beginning of an existing array.

It takes two arguments to specify the name of the array and the value that will become the new element. The value to be added can be defined as a string, a number or a scalar.

Multiple new leading elements can also be added by specifying the value to be added as another array.

The Perl "shift()" function just takes the array name as its argument and will remove the first element of that array.

In this example an array of three elements is first created. Then the "unshift()" function adds a new first element. Finally, the "shift()" function removes the new first element:

unshift.pl

The "shift()" function returns the removed element value. This can be assigned to a scalar in the same way as the "pop()" function in the example on the facing page.

```perl
#!/usr/bin/perl

@arr = ("tue","wed","thu");

print "Content-type:text/html\n\n";
print "<html><ul>";
print "<li>Original array is :@arr";

unshift(@arr,"mon");
print "<li>Array is now : @arr";

shift(@arr);
print "<li>Array is back to : @arr";

print "</ul></html>";
```

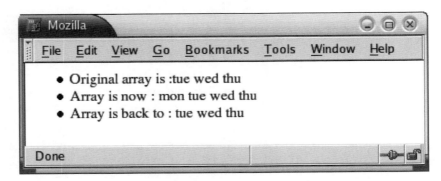

- Original array is :tue wed thu
- Array is now : mon tue wed thu
- Array is back to : tue wed thu

Add/remove last element

The PERL "push()" function adds to the end of an existing array and the "pop()" function removes the final element.

They work just like "unshift()" and "shift()" functions do except they perform at the end of an array.

In the example below "push()" adds the elements of a second array onto the end of those already in the original array. Then "pop()" removes the last element and stores its value:

pushpop.pl

```perl
#!/usr/bin/perl

@count = (1..5);
@extra = (6..10);

print "Content-type:text/html\n\n";
print "<html><ul>";
print "<li>First Half : @count";

push(@count, @extra);
print "<li>Full Count : @count";

$store = pop(@count);
print "<li>One Removed : @count";
print "<li>Removed Value : $store";

print "</ul></html>";
```

This example uses the Range operator to fill both sets of array elements. See page 41 for details.

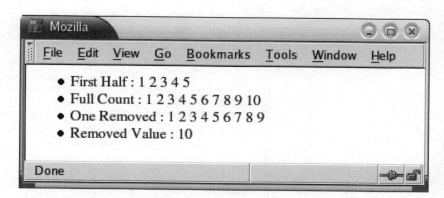

- First Half : 1 2 3 4 5
- Full Count : 1 2 3 4 5 6 7 8 9 10
- One Removed : 1 2 3 4 5 6 7 8 9
- Removed Value : 10

Combining arrays

Multiple arrays can be assigned to a new array to create an array with their combined element values.

The arrays to be assigned must be contained within brackets and separated by a comma.

In this example the script first creates two arrays with three elements in each array. These are then assigned to a new array to create an array with their combined element values.

The combined element values are shown in a HTML table:

combine.pl

```
#!/usr/bin/perl

@arr1 = ("cat","dog","bird");
@arr2 = ("man","woman","child");
@combined = (@arr1,@arr2);

print << "DOC";
Content-type:text/html\n\n
<html>
<table border="2" cellpadding="2">
<tr><td align="center">
<b>Combined Arrays:</b><br>
@combined </td></tr></table>
</html>

DOC
```

More than two arrays can be combined with this process. For example, 3 arrays can be combined with @com=(@arr1,@arr2,@arr3)

Replacing elements

Individual element values can be replaced by addressing the element and simply assigning a new value to it.

Multiple element values can be replaced using their array index numbers separated by a comma.

The assignations must be within brackets and also separated by a comma.

In the following example an array first has a single element value replaced, then multiple element values are replaced:

replace.pl

```perl
#!/usr/bin/perl

@arr = ("cat","dog","bird");

print "Content-type:text/html\n\n";
print "<html><ul>";
print "<li>Original array is :@arr";

$arr[0] = "burger";
print "<li>Amended array is : @arr";

@arr[1,2] = ("and","fries");
print "<li>Final array is : @arr";

print "</ul></html>";
```

The elements need not be consecutive so any index numbers can be specified – and in any order.

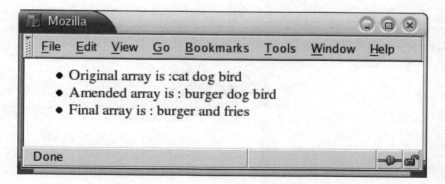

Sorting elements

The PERL "sort" function can be used to alphabetically arrange the element values of an array.

This function is followed by curly brackets that contain a comparison routine to sort the element values.

For comparison, the element values are temporarily passed to scalars named **$a** and **$b** then the "cmp" operator performs the alphabetical comparison.

The "sort" function does not directly change the original array elements but the sorted element values can be assigned to a new array.

This example illustrates both forward and backward sorting:

sort-alpha.pl

```perl
#!/usr/bin/perl

@pets = ("cat","dog","bird","animals");
@petsfwd = sort{$a cmp $b}@pets;
@petsback = sort{$b cmp $a}@pets;

print "Content-type:text/html\n\n";
print "<html><ul>";
print "<li>The pets are: @pets";

print "<li>Alphabetically: @petsfwd";

print "<li>Reverse Order: @petsback";

print "</ul></html>";
```

For more details on the "cmp" operator see page 38.

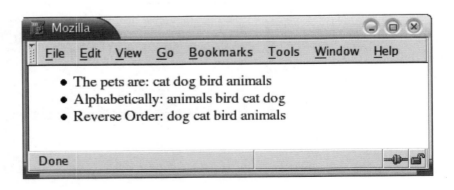

PERL's "sort" function can also be used to arrange the numerical element values of an array.

The operation works in precisely the same manner as the alphabetical sorting example on the facing page.

Again the element values are temporarily passed to scalars named **$a** and **$b** for comparison but now the "<=>" operator performs the numerical comparison.

The sorted element values can be assigned to a new array but the "sort" function does not directly change the original array elements.

Here the example shows ascending and descending sorting:

sort-num.pl

For more details on the "<=>" operator see page 38.

```perl
#!/usr/bin/perl

@nums = (3,1,6,2,10,7,4,9,5,8);
@nums1 = sort{$a <=> $b}@nums;
@nums2 = sort{$b <=> $a}@nums;

print "Content-type:text/html\n\n";
print "<html><ul>";
print "<li>The numbers are: @nums";

print "<li>Ascending Order: @nums1";

print "<li>Descending Order: @nums2";

print "</ul></html>";
```

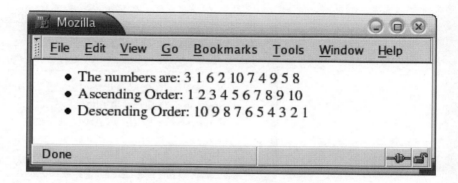

Slice and reverse

Using multiple selected elements from an array is referred to as taking a "slice" of the array.

The syntax to take a "slice" has the index numbers of the selected elements, separated by commas, inside the square brackets that follow the array name.

In the example script on this page the code takes a slice from the "@arr" array and assigns it to the new array "@slice".

To show how the order of array elements can be reversed, the example then demonstrates the PERL "reverse()" function.

The reversed slice is assigned to a new array "@rev" and all three arrays are displayed by the HTML code:

slice-rev.pl

The "qw()" function means that the element values do not need any surrounding quotes.

```perl
#!/usr/bin/perl

@arr = qw(Andrew James David William);
@slice = @arr[0,3];
@rev = reverse(@slice);

print "Content-type:text/html\n\n";
print "<html><ul>";
print "<li>Names : @arr";

print "<li>Slice is : @slice";

print "<li>Reverse is : @rev";

print "</ul></html>";
```

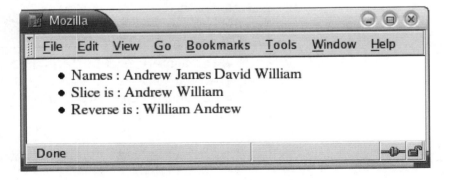

Using hashes

This chapter is devoted to the hash variable. A hash variable is extremely useful for handling HTML form data when it is submitted to a web server from a browser. It is a special type of variable that arranges its data in pairs to form an "associative array". Examples demonstrate how to manipulate hash data pairs in PERL scripts.

Covers

Chapter Six

Key-value pairs

Hash variables are a special type of array variable that store data in associated pairs. This is known as an "associative array".

This is a particularly useful variable for handling HTML form data when it is sent from the web page to a PERL script on the server. The form data is sent as pairs in which the key is the form field name and the value is the data in that field.

The "o"s in the "%" symbol are a reminder of the pairs inside hash arrays.

A hash array is declared using the "%" symbol followed by a given name – with the usual variable naming conventions.

PERL can access the associated value of a hash pair by specifying its key name.

The syntax to access a single hash value requires that the "$" character be placed in front of the hash name. The required key name is specified in curly brackets following the hash name.

This example creates a hash containing two pairs then the HTML code displays the values associated with the key names:

key-values.pl

```
#!C:\Perl\bin\perl

%hsh = ("bird","Swan","fish","Trout");

print "Content-type:text/html\n\n";
print "<html><ul>";
print "<li>Bird is $hsh{\"bird\"}";
print "<li>Fish is $hsh{\"fish\"}";
print "</ul></html>";
```

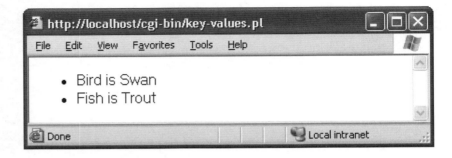

Hash slices

A slice of selected hash variables can be assigned in a similar way to that of a regular array.

The only difference is that the value's key is used to address each required element instead of using an index number.

Hash key names that are integers do not need to be enclosed in quotes when addressing their associated values.

When referencing a hash slice the "@" symbol must precede the hash key name in order to address multiple values.

The hash key name is followed by curly brackets containing the required hash key names. All the key names must be enclosed in quotes and separated by a comma.

The example below defines a hash array then assigns two slices from it to new array variables:

hash-slice.pl

```
#!C:\Perl\bin\perl

%hsh = qw( r red g green b blue );

@slice1 = @hsh{"r","b"};
@slice2 = @hsh{"g","r"};

print "Content-type:text/html\n\n";
print "<html><ul>";
print "<li>Slice 1 is @slice1 ";
print "<li>Slice 2 is @slice2 ";
print "</ul></html>";
```

Getting all keys

The PERL "keys()" function is useful to get all the key names from inside a hash array.

A single argument is required with this function to specify the name of the hash to get the key names from.

This example first creates two hash arrays whose elements are then concatenated into a new third array called "%both".

The key name of each pair is displayed by the HTML code.

get-keys.pl

```
#!C:\Perl\bin\perl

%hsh1 = qw( R Red G Green B Blue );
%hsh2 = qw( Y Yellow P Purple );
%both = ( %hsh1, %hsh2 );

@arr1 = keys(%hsh1);
@arr2 = keys(%hsh2);
@allkeys = keys(%both);

print "Content-type:text/html\n\n";
print "<html><ul>";
print "<li>Hash 1 keys are @arr1";
print "<li>Hash 2 keys are @arr2";
print "<li>Combined keys: @allkeys";
print "</ul></html>";
```

The order of the elements is not maintained as the "@arr1" array does not store the key names in the given order of R,G,B.

Getting all values

The PERL "values()" function is a similar function to the "keys()" function.

All the values in a hash array can be retrieved using the "values()" function.

The hash name that contains the required values is specified as the single argument to the "values()" function.

The example displays the values of each pair:

get-values.pl

```
#!C:\Perl\bin\perl

%hsh1 = qw( R Red G Green B Blue );
%hsh2 = qw( Y Yellow P Purple );
%both = ( %hsh1, %hsh2 );

@arr1 = values( %hsh1 );
@arr2 = values( %hsh2 );
@allvals = values( %both );

print "Content-type:text/html\n\n";
print "<html><ul>";
print "<li>Hash 1 values are: @arr1";
print "<li>Hash 2 values are @arr2";
print "<li>All values are: @allvals";
print "</ul></html>";
```

Although the pairs may not be in their original order the keys are still associated with their proper values.

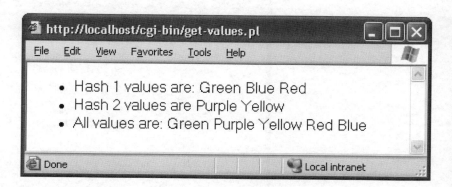

http://localhost/cgi-bin/get-values.pl

File   Edit   View   Favorites   Tools   Help

- Hash 1 values are: Green Blue Red
- Hash 2 values are Purple Yellow
- All values are: Green Purple Yellow Red Blue

Done   Local intranet

Getting all keys and values

The previous two examples that get keys and values from a hash array can be combined in a loop.

A "foreach" loop gets each successive key and its associated value on each iteration.

The example uses the code from the earlier examples to loop through each key, then display the key name and its value:

get-keys-and-values.pl

```
#!C:\Perl\bin\perl

%hsh1 = qw( R Red G Green B Blue );
%hsh2 = qw( Y Yellow P Purple );
%both = ( %hsh1, %hsh2 );

print "Content-type:text/html\n\n";
print "<html><ul>";

foreach $key ( keys(%both) )
{
  print "<li>Key is $key
  and Value is $both{$key}"
}

print "</ul></html>";
```

A "foreach" loop is like a "for" loop that repeats as long as there is another key on the array.

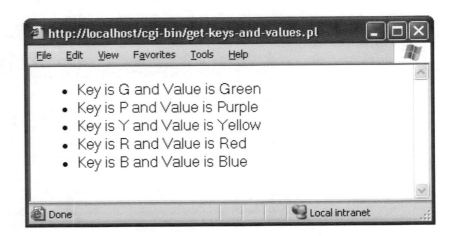

http://localhost/cgi-bin/get-keys-and-values.pl

File   Edit   View   Favorites   Tools   Help

- Key is G and Value is Green
- Key is P and Value is Purple
- Key is Y and Value is Yellow
- Key is R and Value is Red
- Key is B and Value is Blue

Done   Local intranet

Deleting pairs

The PERL "delete" keyword can be used to remove pairs from within a hash array.

Address the pair to be deleted with the key name enclosed in curly brackets after the hash name.

The hash name should be preceded by a "$" character to denote that a single element is being addressed.

In this example the script deletes two of the pairs from the hash array using the example on the opposite page:

delete.pl

```
#!C:\Perl\bin\perl

%hsh1 = qw( R Red G Green B Blue );
%hsh2 = qw( Y Yellow P Purple );
%both = ( %hsh1, %hsh2 );

delete $both{"Y"};
delete $both{"G"};

print "Content-type:text/html\n\n";
print "<html><ul>";

foreach $key (keys (%both))
{
  print "<li>Key is $key
  and Value is $both{$key}"
}

print "</ul></html>";
```

The value of a deleted pair can be assigned to a scalar variable if required with
$saved= delete{"keyname"}.

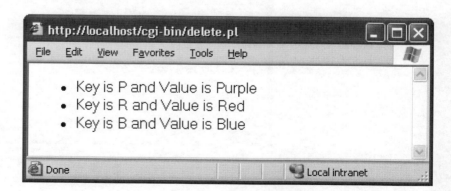

http://localhost/cgi-bin/delete.pl

- Key is P and Value is Purple
- Key is R and Value is Red
- Key is B and Value is Blue

Confirm key existence

It is often useful to check a hash array to determine if a particular key exists in order to branch the script.

The PERL "exists" keyword will search a hash array for a key name and return a value of 1 if the key is found.

If the key is not found the "exists" keyword returns 0 – although this may not be apparent unless tested for.

This example specifies the value of a string depending on the result of the search to illustrate this point:

exists.pl

```
#!C:\Perl\bin\perl

%hsh1 = qw( R Red G Green B Blue );
%hsh2 = qw( Y Yellow P Purple );
%both = ( %hsh1, %hsh2 );

$check_p = exists $both{"P"};
$check_t = exists $both{"T"};
$num = ( $check_t == 0 ) ? "zero" : "one";

print "Content-type:text/html\n\n";
print "<html><ul>";
print "<li>Does P exist ? $check_p";
print "<li>Does T exist ? $check_t";
print "<li>Check \"T\" is $num";
print "</ul></html>";
```

Use an "exists" test with an "if" statement to perform an action if the key is located in the hash.

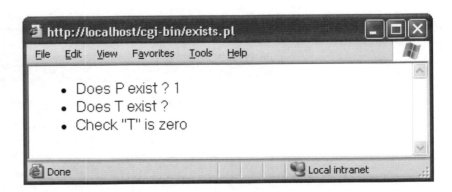

http://localhost/cgi-bin/exists.pl

File   Edit   View   Favorites   Tools   Help

- Does P exist ? 1
- Does T exist ?
- Check "T" is zero

Done   Local intranet

Subroutines

This chapter describes, by example, how subroutines can be useful to define pieces of code that can be repeatedly used in a PERL script.

Covers

Chapter Seven

Defining a subroutine

A "subroutine" is the name for a PERL function that can be called repeatedly from within the main script to execute a statement, or several statements.

It is customary to define the subroutines at the end of the main body of the script.

A subroutine is defined with the PERL keyword "sub" followed by a given name for the subroutine. This name should follow the naming conventions used for variables.

The statements to be executed are contained in curly brackets after the subroutine name.

This example defines a subroutine at the end of the script but it is never called in the main body of the script:

define-sub.pl

```perl
#!/usr/bin/perl

print "Content-type:text/html\n\n";
print "<html><h2>Subroutines</h2><ul>";

print "<li>A line from the script";

print "</ul></html>";

# define a subroutine...
sub greet
{
    print "<li>Hi from the subroutine!";
}
```

Calling a subroutine

A subroutine can be called to execute its statements from any point within the main body of the PERL script.

To make the call an ampersand character is used in front of the subroutine name.

It is considered good style to use subroutines widely where a particular action is repeated in the script. Subroutines may perform quite complex actions and can be regarded almost as a "script within a script".

The example below builds on the example on the opposite page by adding two calls to the defined subroutine:

call-sub.pl

```perl
#!/usr/bin/perl

print "Content-type:text/html\n\n";
print "<html><h2>Subroutines</h2><ul>";

&greet;
print "<li>A line from the script";
&greet;

print "</ul></html>";

sub greet
{
    print "<li>Hi from the subroutine!";
}
```

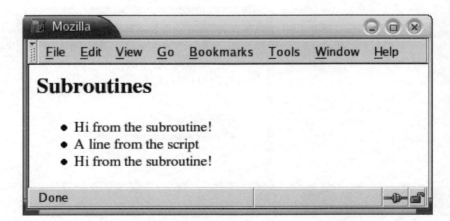

Passing values to a subroutine

Like other functions a PERL subroutine can be passed a value as an argument from the caller.

The argument as usual is contained in regular brackets that follow the subroutine name in the function call.

PERL automatically stores the arguments passed in a special array called the "underscore array" – which is addressed as "@_".

The first argument value is placed in the underscore array's first element and can be referenced with the syntax @_[0].

In the following example a subroutine is defined that will display the value of the single argument passed by the caller:

pass-value.pl

When only a single argument is passed to the underscore array it can also be addressed as "@_" as well as "$@_[0]".

```perl
#!/usr/bin/perl

print "Content-type:text/html\n\n";
print "<html><h2>Subroutines</h2><ul>";

&showvalue("Gold");

print "<li>A line from the script";
print "</ul></html>";

sub showvalue
{
    print "<li>Metal is $_[0]";
}
```

The caller to a subroutine can pass multiple values to the subroutine as arguments separated by a comma.

These argument values are stored in the special underscore array in sequential elements. So the first value is stored at **@_[0]**, the second value at **@_[1]**, and so on.

The example below builds on the single value example on the previous page to now pass two values.

In this example a subroutine is defined that will display both values of the two arguments passed by the caller:

pass-values.pl

```perl
#!/usr/bin/perl

print "Content-type:text/html\n\n";
print "<html><h2>Subroutines</h2><ul>";

&showvalue("Gold","Silver");

print "<li>A line from the script";
print "</ul></html>";

sub showvalue
{
    print "<li>Metal is $_[0]";
    print "<li>Metal is $_[1]";
}
```

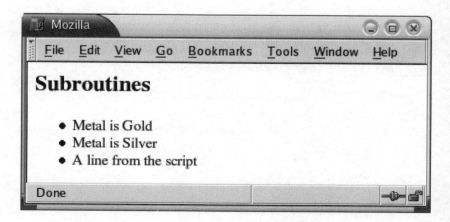

Library files

The subroutines in a PERL script may be placed in a separate file called a library. Library files are text files that contain the subroutines and normally have the ".lib" file extension.

The library file does not need a "she-bang" line but must always end with a final "1" to return **true** to the parser.

This example library is saved with the filename "subs.lib":

subs.lib

```perl
sub mimetype
{
    print "Content-type:text/html\n\n";
}

sub dochead
{
    print "<html><h4> $_[0] </h4>";
}

sub start_table
{
    print "<table border=2><tr><td>";
}

sub end_table
{
    print "</td><tr></table>";
}

sub showvalue
{
    print "<li>Metal is $_[0]";
}

sub docfoot
{
    print "</html>";
}

1
```

The final "1" confirms that the file was successfully accessed.

The library file must be located where PERL can find it. Examples can be placed in Apache's /cgi-bin directory.

Calling a library subroutine

In order for a PERL script to use a library the name of the library must be defined at the start of the script using the PERL "require" keyword.

The example below first defines that the script can use the library described on the facing page called "subs.lib".

The subroutines are then called in the usual way.

call-lib.pl

```perl
#!/usr/bin/perl

require "subs.lib";

&mimetype;

&dochead("Subroutines Library");

&start_table;

&showvalue("Gold");

&showvalue("Silver");

&showvalue("Bronze");

&end_table;

print "<li>A line from the script";

&docfoot;
```

Notice that the keyword is "require", and not "requires".

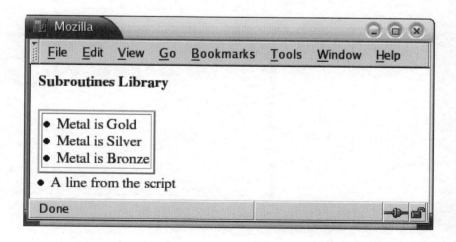

Returning a value

The PERL "return" keyword is used in subroutines to return a final value to the caller of that subroutine.

In the example on this page the subroutine caller passes two integer values as arguments to the subroutine. These integers are stored in the special underscore array.

The subroutine executes its code statements then the final value is returned to the caller using the "return" keyword.

This returned value is assigned to a scalar, then displayed.

return.pl

```perl
#!/usr/bin/perl

$number = 5;
$multiplier = 100;
$result = calc($number,$multiplier);

print "Content-type:text/html\n\n";
print "<html>";
print "<h4>Return Sub Value</h4>";
print "The result is $result";
print "</html>";

sub calc
{
    $sum = $_[0] * $_[1];
    return $sum;
}
```

HOT TIP

Unless specified with the "return" keyword, the default return value is that of the final expression evaluated in the statement block. So using **sub calc{ $_[0] * $_[1] }** *could replace the subroutine in this example.*

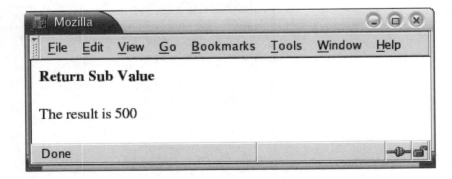

PERL functions

This chapter illustrates how intrinsic PERL functions can be used in scripts. Time and currency formatting are demonstrated along with random number generation. Further examples also explore other useful functions.

Covers

Chapter Eight

Random number generator

The PERL "rand" function takes a single numeric argument and returns a random floating number between zero and the value of its argument.

The random number in this example will be between zero and 10 – but not equal to or greater than 10.

The PERL "int" function gets the integer part of the floating number by truncating the number at the decimal point.

rand.pl

```
#!C:\Perl\bin\perl

$num = rand(10);
$int = int($num);

for( $i=0; $i<6; $i++ )
{
    $seq[$i] = int(rand(49)) + 1;
}

print "Content-type:text/html\n\n";
print "<html><ul>";
print "<b>Random Numbers</b>";
print "<li>0-9 random is $num";
print "<li>Integer part is $int";
print "<li>Sequence is @seq";
print "</ul></html>";
```

The example loop fills an array with six random numbers. By adding 1 to the returned integer the range will be between 1 and 49 inclusive.

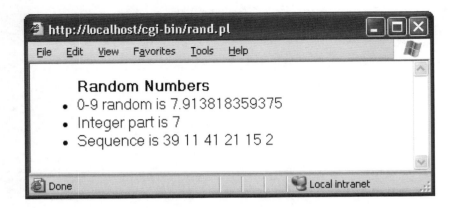

http://localhost/cgi-bin/rand.pl

File   Edit   View   Favorites   Tools   Help

Random Numbers
- 0-9 random is 7.913818359375
- Integer part is 7
- Sequence is 39 11 41 21 15 2

Done   Local intranet

The PERL "int" function can also be useful to truncate random numbers if shorter floating numbers are required.

The example below creates a floating number between zero and 50, then truncates it to two decimal places.

The random number is multiplied by 100 and the rest of the number is removed at the decimal point.

Dividing this truncated value by 100 leaves a floating number to two decimal places.

rand-float.pl

```
#!C:\Perl\bin\perl

$num = rand(50);
$tmp = $num * 100;
$int = int($tmp);
$flt = $int / 100;

print "Content-type:text/html\n\n";
print "<html><ul>";
print "<li>0-50 random = $num";
print "<li>Multiplied x 100 = $tmp";
print "<li>Integer part = $int";
print "<li>Truncated float is $flt";
print "</ul></html>";
```

Random numbers can be useful to generate web page banners in a random manner.

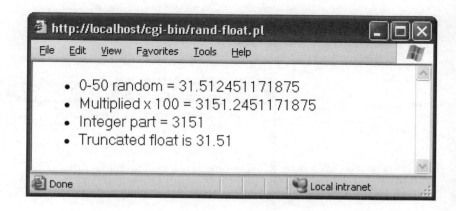

- 0-50 random = 31.512451171875
- Multiplied x 100 = 3151.2451171875
- Integer part = 3151
- Truncated float is 31.51

Formatting data

In addition to the standard "print" function PERL can format the output data by using the "printf" function.

This function takes two arguments to specify the type of formatting required, and the data to be formatted.

The second argument that specifies the data to be formatted can be a scalar variable.

The formatting type specified in the first argument always starts with a "%" character followed by the format required, and should be enclosed in quotes.

For instance, formatting to force data to have at least four integer digits is specified with "%4d". To ensure that leading zeros are inserted this becomes "%04d".

The example below demonstrates the "printf" function formatting output. Also illustrated is the "sprintf" function that works in just the same way but is used when saving the formatted data to a scalar variable.

format.pl

```
#!C:\Perl\bin\perl

$savedformatted = sprintf("%04d",8);

print "Content-type:text/html\n\n";
print "<html><ul>";
print "<li>Direct Formatted Output:";
printf("%04d",256);
print "<li>Saved Formatted Output:";
print "$savedformatted";
print "</ul></html>";
```

Formatting currency

The "printf" and "sprintf" functions introduced on the opposite page are commonly used to format currency sums.

Floating-point numbers can be formatted to force data to contain a specific number of decimal places.

These will be filled with zeros where needed.

For instance, to force data to always have two decimal places formatting is specified with "%.2f".

This formatting is useful to add zeros to the right side of currency amounts – so that "$7.50" does not become "$7.5".

In the following example the "sprintf" function saves a formatted currency sum to a scalar variable that is displayed by the HTML code. Also the "printf" function is demonstrated directly formatting a currency output value.

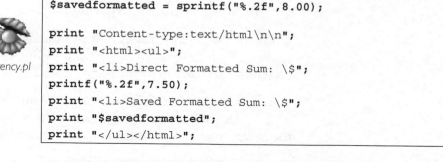

currency.pl

```
#!C:\Perl\bin\perl

$savedformatted = sprintf("%.2f",8.00);

print "Content-type:text/html\n\n";
print "<html><ul>";
print "<li>Direct Formatted Sum: \$";
printf("%.2f",7.50);
print "<li>Saved Formatted Sum: \$";
print "$savedformatted";
print "</ul></html>";
```

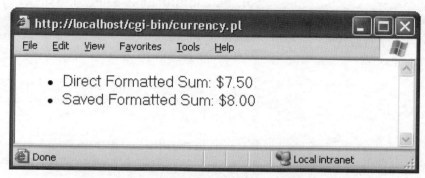

```
http://localhost/cgi-bin/currency.pl
File   Edit   View   Favorites   Tools   Help
```

- Direct Formatted Sum: $7.50
- Saved Formatted Sum: $8.00

Done   Local intranet

Handling time

PERL has a number of useful features to handle time and date which are demonstrated in the example on the opposite page.

The "time" keyword returns the current time in milliseconds from the system clock. This can be translated to local time and date information using the "localtime" function. Alternatively, the "gmtime" function can translate it to date and time information at Greenwich Mean Time (Universal Time).

The eight parts of the time data are always returned in this order so need to be assigned accordingly.

All eight individual components of either time function can be assigned to scalar variables using the syntax on lines 6 and 7.

The example uses the "localtime" function returns but could equally have assigned the returns from the "gmtime" function if the data is required to be in the GMT time format.

Most of the scalar variables will receive straightforward values but some need adjustment for meaningful use.

The **$mon** variable gets the month of the year starting at zero for January up to 11 for December. This value should be incremented for normal use so that January is month 1.

Similarly, the **$yday** scalar gets the day number of the year, again counting from zero at January 1st. This value should also be incremented so the first day of the year is day 1.

The **$year** variable gets a count starting from 1900. So for the year 2005, the **$year** value is 105. To realize the actual year the value in the **$year** variable must be added to the value 1900.

The time information assigned to the **$hour**, **$min** and **$sec** scalars can be formatted to be always two digits using the PERL "sprintf" function. For instance, this would display a value of five minutes as "05" rather than just "5".

Two arguments are required by the "sprintf" function to specify the type of formatting, "%02d" for two digits, and the name of the scalar to be formatted.

If the time returned occurs during daylight savings time, the **$isdst** scalar receives a **true** value of 1. Otherwise this variable will get a **false** value of zero.

time.pl

The code assigning the time components would normally be on a single line – it is only split over two lines here due to space limitations.

```perl
#!C:\Perl\bin\perl

$servertime = localtime(time); # get local time
$gmt = gmtime(time);            # get universal time

($sec, $min, $hour, $mday, $mon, $year, $wday, $yday,
$isdst) = localtime(time);      # get time components

$mon++;                         # correct month to 1-12
$yday++;                        # correct day to 1-365
$year += 1900;                  # correct year
$hour = sprintf("%02d",$hour);  # format hours
$min = sprintf("%02d", $min);   # format minutes
$sec = sprintf("%02d", $sec);   # format seconds
$ds = ($isdst == 1) ? "Yes":"No"; # get daylight saving

print << "DOC";
Content-type:text/html\n\n
<html><ul>      <li>Server time: $servertime
                <li>Universal time: $gmt
                <li>Date: $mon-$mday-$year
                <li>Time: $hour:$min:$sec
                <li>Daylight saving: $ds
                <li>Day of the week: $wday
                <li>Day of the year: $yday </ul></html>

DOC
```

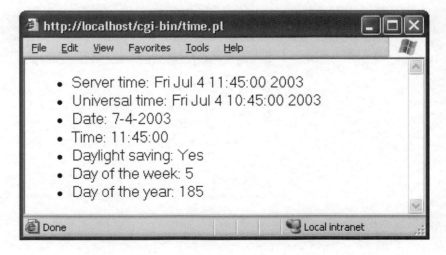

Chopping strings

The PERL "chop" function is used to remove the final character of a text string.

This function returns the character that has just been removed and shortens the original string.

In the example below the **$str** scalar is assigned an initial value that is displayed by the HTML code. Then the "chop" function removes the last character and assigns it to a scalar.

The removed character and the newly shortened string are finally displayed in the HTML code.

chop.pl

```perl
#!C:\Perl\bin\perl

print "Content-type:text/html\n\n";
print "<html><ul><b>Chop...</b>";

$str = "PERL";
print "<li>Original String: $str";

$char = chop( $str );
print "<li>Chopped Character: $char";

$chopstr = $str;
print "<li>Chopped String: $chopstr";

print "<ul></html>";
```

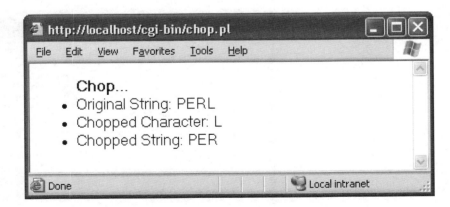

Chomping newlines

Not to be confused with the "chop" function, the PERL "chomp" function is used to safely remove only unseen characters from the end of a string.

Most commonly "chomp" removes the invisible newline characters that have been added by the user.

This example demonstrates the effect that "chomp" has on strings with and without ending newline characters:

chomp.pl

```
#!C:\Perl\bin\perl

print "Content-type:text/html\n\n";
print "<html><ul><b>Chomp...</b>";

$regular = "PERL Script";

$chompit = chomp($regular);
print "<li>Chomp Regular: $regular";
print "<li>Did Chomp: $chompit <hr>";

$with_nl="PERL Script
";

$chompit = chomp($with_nl);
print "<li>Chomp Newline: $with_nl";
print "<li>Did Chomp: $chompit";

print "</ul></html>";
```

It is advisable to "chomp" all user input to avoid problems with unseen characters – like newlines.

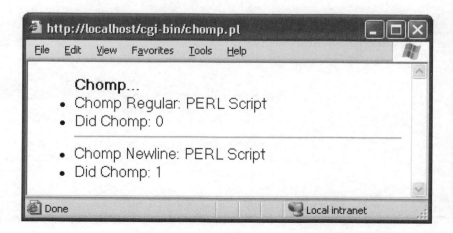

The eval function

The PERL "eval" function is useful to evaluate code statements and trap any errors they may contain.

If the evaluated statements contain a syntax error or a runtime error the "eval" function traps the error.

When errors are trapped a special PERL variable called "$@" is assigned an error message that describes the error.

When no errors are detected "eval" returns a **true** value of 1.

In the example below there is a deliberate syntax error in the statement that is to be evaluated.

The error message locates the error in the first line of the statement block of the first "eval" function in the script.

eval.pl

```perl
#!C:\Perl\bin\perl

$num = 7;
eval ("$num = ;");   # deliberate error

print "Content-type:text/html\n\n";
if ($@ eq "")
{
  print("eval() success");
}
else
{
  print("eval() fail: $@");
}
print "</html>";
```

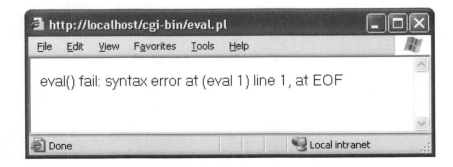

```
http://localhost/cgi-bin/eval.pl

File   Edit   View   Favorites   Tools   Help

eval() fail: syntax error at (eval 1) line 1, at EOF

Done                                    Local intranet
```

Warn and die functions

When the "eval" function detects an error it can be recorded in Apache's error log file using the PERL "warn" function. This catches the error message from the special "$@" variable but allows the script to continue. Alternatively the error can be recorded and the script halted using the "die" function.

In each case, the error message specified as the function argument will be written in the error log. The example below writes a brief description and the error message itself from the "$@" variable.

warn-die.pl

```
#!C:\Perl\bin\perl

print "Content-type:text/html\n\n";
print "<html>Warn...";
eval { alarm(100) }; warn("server warning: $@") if $@ ;

print "Die...";
eval { alarm(100) }; die("stopped: $@") if $@;

print "End.";
eval { alarm(100) }; warn("server warning: $@") if $@;

print "</html>";
```

The final warning in this example is not made because "die" has already stopped the script.

http://localhost/cgi-bin/warn-die.pl

File   Edit   View   Favorites   Tools   Help

Warn...Die...

Done   Local intranet

*In Windows errors are recorded in a file named **error.log** in Apache's **logs** directory. In Linux they are typically recorded in /var/log/httpd/error_log.*

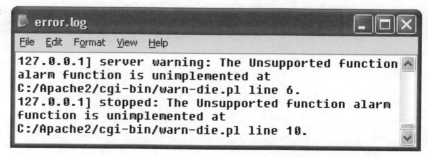

error.log

File   Edit   Format   View   Help

127.0.0.1] server warning: The Unsupported function
alarm function is unimplemented at
C:/Apache2/cgi-bin/warn-die.pl line 6.
127.0.0.1] stopped: The Unsupported function alarm
function is unimplemented at
C:/Apache2/cgi-bin/warn-die.pl line 10.

Packing strings

The PERL "pack" function takes a list of values and converts them into a single string according to the rules specified by its first argument.

Most usually this function will be converting to standard signed characters, for which the rule is the letter "c".

The rule should be repeated for each item in the ensuing list that is to be converted.

This example demonstrates the "pack" function converting a list of ASCII character codes to a text string. Also a list of hexadecimal codes are converted to a text string:

pack.pl

```perl
#!C:\Perl\bin\perl

print "Content-type:text/html\n\n";
print "<html>";

$chrstr = pack("cccc",80,69,82,76);

$hexstr = pack("ccc", hex(0x8f),hex(0x93),hex(0x95));

print "<h2>$chrstr $hexstr scripting</h2>";

print "</html>";
```

The "pack" function is very useful when handling encoded data from a web browser. See the form parser example on page 128 for details.

Pattern matching

This chapter introduces "regular expressions" to search through a string for a specified substring. The examples demonstrate how to perform pattern matching and illustrate how located matches can be manipulated in a variety of useful ways.

Covers

Chapter Nine

Match string

PERL syntax to search a string always requires the string, or its variable name, to be followed by the "=~" binding operator.

The search pattern is defined after the binding operator.

To find a match the "m" (for "match") identifier is needed followed by the pattern to find enclosed by forward slashes.

Optionally the pattern definition can end with an "i" (for "ignore") quantifier to ignore case when searching. This is demonstrated in this example that searches for two matches:

match.pl

There should be no spaces in the search pattern definition.

Notice how much more compact the code is for the second search.

```perl
#!/usr/bin/perl

$str = "She sang 'Shebang!' ";

print "Content-type:text/html\n\n";
print "<html><h4>String: $str</h4><ul>";

if( $str =~ m/she/i )
{
    print "<li>Pattern 'she' matched";
}
else
{
    print "<li>Pattern 'she' not found";
}
$fnd = ( $str =~ m/line/i ) ? "Yes" : "No";
print "<li>Was 'line' found?: $fnd";
print "</ul></html>";
```

View match

There are three special PERL variables that can be used to manipulate text content following a successful match:

- The "$&" ampersand variable contains the actual string that was matched

- The "$`" backtick variable contains all text preceding the matched string

- The "$'" apostrophe variable contains all text following the matched string

This example displays the contents of all three special variables:

view-match.pl

```perl
#!/usr/bin/perl

$str = "She sang 'Shebang!' ";

print "Content-type:text/html\n\n";
print "<html><h4>String: $str</h4><ul>";

$fnd = ( $str =~ m/sang/i ) ? "Yes" : "No";

print "<li>Was 'sang' found?: $fnd";

print "<li>Text before match: $`";
print "<li>Text string matched: $&";
print "<li>Text after match: $'";

print "</ul></html>";
```

The "backtick" character key is often found above the "tab" key on many keyboards.

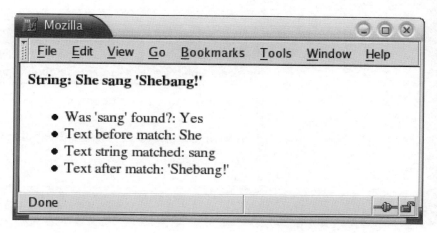

Substitute string

In addition to searching strings for a match to a specified pattern, PERL can replace the match when it has been found.

To replace a match the "s" (for "substitute") identifier is required when defining the search pattern.

The "s" search pattern in this example will only substitute the first match in the searched string.

This is followed by the pattern to find, enclosed by forward slashes as usual, then the string that is to replace the match.

A final forward slash terminates the replacement string and an "i" quantifier can be added if case is to be ignored.

The search pattern should not contain any spaces unless they form part of the pattern itself.

In this example the script searches the original string for the "bang" pattern that it replaces with the new specified text:

substitute.pl

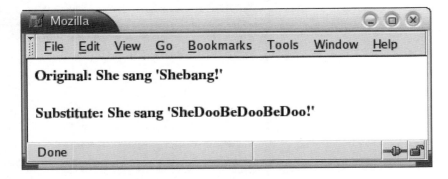

The "s" search is used to substitute spaces for the "+" character in the Form Parser script that is on page 128.

```perl
#!/usr/bin/perl

$str = "She sang 'Shebang!' ";

print "Content-type:text/html\n\n";
print "<html>";
print "<h4>Original: $str</h4>";

$str =~ s/bang/DooBeDooBeDoo/i;

print "<h4>Substitute: $str</h4>";

print "</html>";
```

Mozilla — File Edit View Go Bookmarks Tools Window Help

Original: She sang 'Shebang!'

Substitute: She sang 'SheDooBeDooBeDoo!'

Done

Split pattern

The PERL "split" function defines a search pattern as its first argument to specify at which point a string should be split.

A second argument specifies the name of the string to be searched and split.

The multiple separated strings can then be assigned to an array variable.

In this example a string is split at the common comma delimiter. The separated strings are stored in an array then a loop writes the content of each element to the HTML code.

split-str.pl

The "split" function is used to separate form data in the Form Parser script on page 128.

```perl
#!/usr/bin/perl

$abc = "Alpha,Bravo,Charlie";

print "Content-type:text/html\n\n";
print "<html>";
print "<h4>Original: $abc</h4><ul>";

@letters = split(/,/ ,$abc);

foreach $letter (@letters)
{
    print "<li>$letter";
}

print "</ul></html>";
```

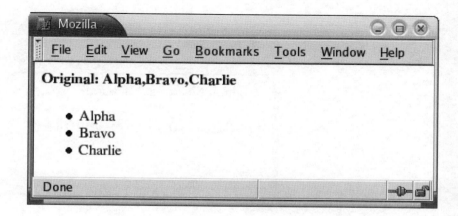

Translate matches

As an alternative to specifying a string to match in a search pattern definition a group of characters may be specified.

This is known as a "class" of characters and the character class is defined between square brackets.

The "tr" search pattern will translate all the matches within the string.

For example a class [1-5] would match all numbers in the range of 1 through 5 inclusive within a searched string.

Multiple ranges can be specified, so the class [a-zA-Z] would match all uppercase and lowercase alphabetical characters.

The example below uses the "tr" (for "translate") search pattern and the class [a-z] to match all lowercase characters.

In this case the match is translated into uppercase characters by specifying the [A-Z] class as the new text.

translate.pl

```perl
#!/usr/bin/perl

$str = "She sang 'Shebang!' ";

print "Content-type:text/html\n\n";
print "<html>";
print "<h4>Original: $str</h4>";

$str =~ tr/[a-z]/[A-Z]/;

print "<h4>Translated: $str</h4>";
print "</html>";
```

The "tr" search is used to translate from hexadecimal in the Form Parser script on page 128.

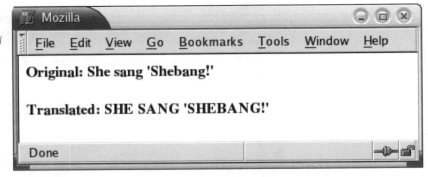

Character classes

The shorthand versions of frequently used character classes are listed in the table below and the example that follows demonstrates one of these in action.

The caret symbol (^) is used to mean a boolean NOT.

Class	Equivalent	Match
\w	[a-zA-Z0-9_]	All letters, digits and underscores
\W	[^a-zA-Z0-9_]	Any characters other than letters, digits or underscores
\d	[0-9]	All digits
\D	[^0-9]	All characters except digits
\s	[\n\t\r\f]	All spaces, new lines, tabs, carriage returns and form feeds
\S	[^\n\t\r\f]	All characters except spaces, new lines, tabs, returns and form feeds

character-classes.pl

```perl
#!/usr/bin/perl

$str = "PERL in easy steps";

print "Content-type:text/html\n\n";
print "<html><b>String: $str</b>";
if( $str =~ m/[\w]/ ){ print "<li>Letters found" }
print "</html>";
```

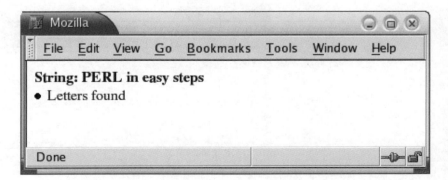

Inclusive and exclusive groups

Pattern matching can be used to determine the direction of a script by conditional branching for seeking included digits.

A search pattern is defined and if a match is found to be included in the searched string the script will follow an affirmative route.

In the example below the search pattern is defined as any digit in the range of zero to 4.

If the search matches any digit in the range 0-4 then the first statement in the statement block will be executed.

inclusive.pl

```perl
#!/usr/bin/perl

$str = "Group 3";

print "Content-type:text/html\n\n";
print "<html><h4>Inclusive</h4>";
print "This group is in the range";

if( $str =~ m/[0-4]/ )
{
    print " 0-4";
}
else
{
    print " 5-9";
}
print "</html>";
```

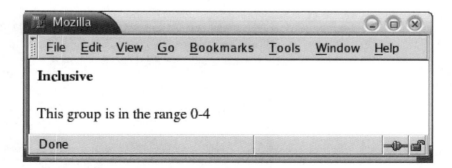

Conditional branching can be performed with pattern matching by searching for excluded digits.

A search pattern is defined and if a match is found to be excluded from the searched string the script will follow a negative route.

In the following example the search pattern is defined as any digit not in the range of zero to 4.

If the search does not match a digit in the range 0-4 then the second statement in the statement block will be executed.

exclusive.pl

```perl
#!/usr/bin/perl

$str = "Group 3";

print "Content-type:text/html\n\n";
print "<html><h4>Exclusive</h4>";
print "This group is in the range";

if( $str =~ m/^[0-4]/ )
{
    print " 5-9";
}
else
{
    print " 0-4";
}
print "</html>";
```

The caret symbol (^) is used as a boolean NOT operator.

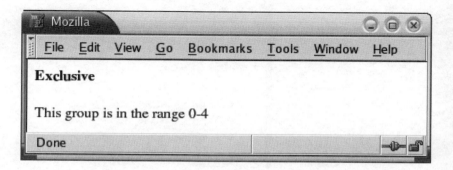

Limited matching

In order to limit the matches to be only an exact match, qualifiers can be added to the search pattern definition.

The example below adds a caret symbol " ^ " in front of the search pattern. The search will then only match if the pattern appears at the start of the searched string.

Also the example adds a dollar symbol "$" after the search pattern. This ensures that the search will only match if the pattern appears at the end of the searched string.

limited.pl

If the example only added the ^ caret qualifier "Hammer" would match. If the example only added the $ dollar qualifier "Wham" would match.

```perl
#!/usr/bin/perl

$ham = "Ham"; $wham = "Wham"; $hammer = "Hammer";
$ok = "Matched"; $no = "No Match";

print "Content-type: text/html\n\n";
print "<html><h4>Limited Match</h4><ul>";

$res = ( $ham =~ m/^Ham$/i ) ? $ok : $no;
{ print "<li>$ham : $res" }

$res = ( $wham =~ m/^Ham$/i ) ? $ok : $no;
{ print "<li>$wham : $res" }

$res = ( $hammer =~ m/^Ham$/i ) ? $ok : $no;
{ print "<li>$hammer : $res" }

print "</ul></html>";
```

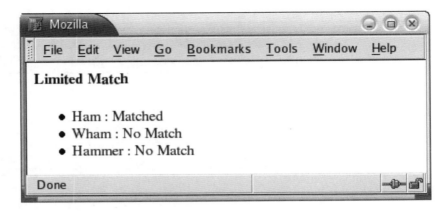

Optional matching

Using a "?" qualifier after a search pattern enables the search to report a match whether the match is made or not.

It is important to note that the "?" qualifier will normally only work with the single character immediately before it.

The search pattern must be enclosed in brackets for the "?" qualifier to work with the whole pattern.

This example matches both searches even though the pattern in the second search is not actually in the searched string:

optional.pl

```perl
#!/usr/bin/perl

$str = "She sang 'Shebang!'";
$ok = "Matched";
$no = "No Match";

print "Content-type:text/html\n\n";
print "<html><h4>Optional Match</h4><ul>";

print "<li>String: $str";

$res = ( $str =~ m/(she)?/i ) ? $ok : $no;
{ print "<li>She : $res" }

$res = ( $str =~ m/(shout)?/i )? $ok : $no;
{ print "<li>Shout : $res" }

print "</ul></html>";
```

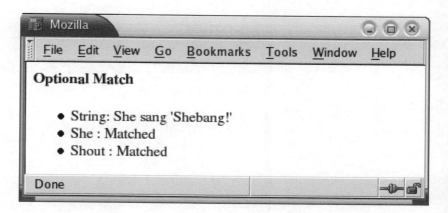

Minimum match

In cases where multiple matches are possible the "+" qualifier can be added after a search pattern to specify that the search must make at least one match.

This example assigns the search pattern to a variable then calls a subroutine to make the search and display the results.

minimum.pl

```perl
#!/usr/bin/perl

$str = "She sang 'Shebang!'";

print "Content-type:text/html\n\n";
print "<html>";
print "<h4>Match At Least Once</h4><ul>";
print "<li>String: $str";

$exp = "She";
&report;

$exp = "Shout";
&report;

print "</ul></html>";

sub report()
{
    $res = ( $str =~ m/($exp)+/ );
    print "<li>$exp : Found"  if $res == 1;
    print "<li>$exp : Failed" if $res != 1;
}
```

The qualifier will only apply to the single character preceding it unless the regular expression is enclosed in brackets.

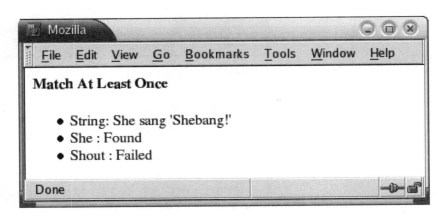

Alternative match

A search definition can specify more than one pattern to search for by separating each pattern with the "|" operator.

The first search in the example below matches the second specified pattern. The second search matches neither of its specified patterns.

alternative.pl

```perl
#!/usr/bin/perl

$str = "She sang 'Shebang!'";
$i = 1;

print "Content-type:text/html\n\n";
print "<html><h4>Alternative Matches</h4><ul>";
print "<li>String: $str";

$res = ( $str =~ m/Shout|She/ );
&report;

$res = ( $str =~ m/Shout|Sham/ );
&report;

print "</ul></html>";

sub report()
{
  if($res == 1){ print "<li>Search $i : \"$&\" Found" }
  else { print "<li>Search $i : No Matches" }
  $i++;
}
```

This example numbers each search from a counter variable that has been initialized at the beginning of the script then is incremented by each search.

Nested strings must have their quotes escaped to avoid the string being prematurely terminated.

Multiple matches

Adding a "g" (for "global") qualifier to the end of the search definition allows multiple matches to be stored in an array.

This example searches for three patterns then assigns the matches to an array.

Finally a loop displays the contents of each element.

multi-match.pl

The search in this example finds two instances of "She" in the searched string so each instance is assigned to an array element.

```perl
#!/usr/bin/perl

$str = "She sang 'Shebang!'";

print "Content-type:text/html\n\n";
print "<html>";
print "<h4>Multiple Matches</h4><ul>";
print "<li>String: $str";

@match = ( $str =~ m/shout|she|bang/ig );
$length = @match;

for( $i = 0; $i < $length; $i++ )
{
        print "<li>Matched : $match[$i]";
}
print "</ul></html>";
```

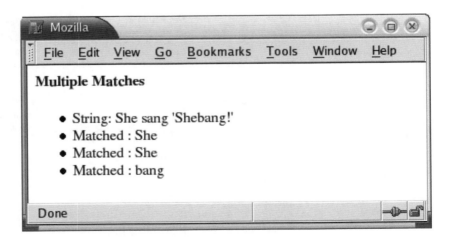

PERL from web pages

This exciting chapter illustrates how web pages can interact with PERL scripts. Different methods of sending data from the browser to the server are demonstrated. The form "parser" is detailed in full and examples show how it can send data back to the browser.

Covers

Chapter Ten

Hyperlinks to PERL

The exciting use of PERL scripts for CGI creates a two-way exchange between the HTML code on the browser page and the PERL code on the web server.

This allows the browser to communicate with a PERL script located in Apache's **cgi-bin** directory using the HTTP protocol. The location on the local system for the examples given throughout this book is **C:\Apache2\cgi-bin** on Windows and **/var/www/cgi-bin** on Linux.

The simplest way to communicate with a CGI script is via a hyperlink in the HTML code. When the user follows that link the PERL script will be called and its code will be executed.

The URL syntax for hyperlinks to CGI scripts follows the standard pattern of protocol, domain name and file name. Using the default name of **localhost** the URL to a script named **hello.pl** would look like this:

```
http://localhost/cgi-bin/hello.pl
```

This URL can be assigned to the **href** attribute of a HTML anchor tag to make the script the target of a hyperlink. This URL is made the target of the link in the HTML document listed below. When the user follows the link the **hello.pl** script is executed and its generated output appears in the browser window.

hello.html

```
<html>

<head>
  <title>Target a PERL script</title>
</head>

<body>
 <p>

  <a href="http://localhost/cgi-bin/hello.pl">Click</a>

 </p>
</body>

</html>
```

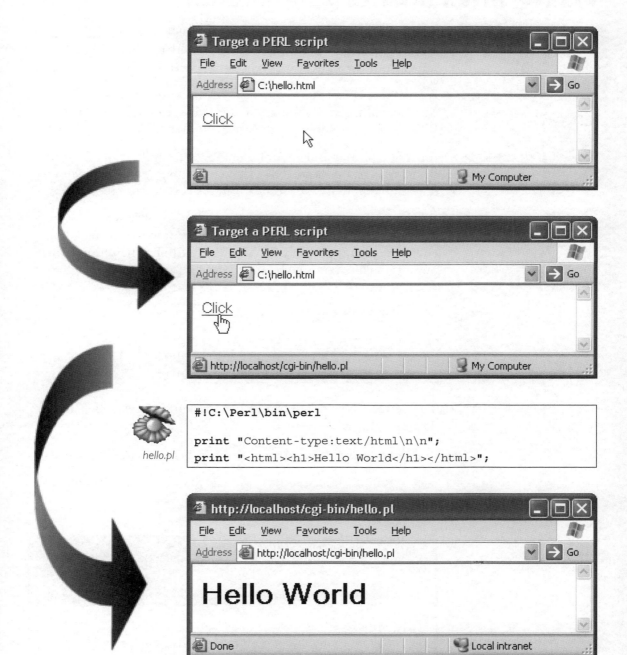

```
#!C:\Perl\bin\perl

print "Content-type:text/html\n\n";
print "<html><h1>Hello World</h1></html>";
```

hello.pl

Using environment variables

Each time a web browser communicates with a web server it passes certain data about itself to the server. This data is stored by the server as "environment variables" in a special hash variable called **%ENV**.

Uppercase characters are always used when addressing the environment variables.

The individual environment variable values can be accessed from a PERL script by addressing their **%ENV** hash keys.

A list of typical useful environment variables appears on the inside front cover of this book. Note that environment variables will vary depending on the server software and data sent from the browser.

It is sometimes useful for a PERL script to establish which browser is being used to call the script. This information is available in the environment variable **HTTP_USER_AGENT**. The script below outputs details about the browser when it is executed.

browser.pl

```
#!C:\Perl\bin\perl

print "Content-type:text/html\n\n";
print "<html><b>Browser Is...</b></br>";
print "$ENV{'HTTP_USER_AGENT'} </html>";
```

This script can be called from a hyperlink in HTML code to display the browser details.

```
<a href="http://localhost/cgi-bin/browser.pl">Click</a>
```

The output illustrated in this case describes Internet Explorer 6 running on a Windows XP platform.

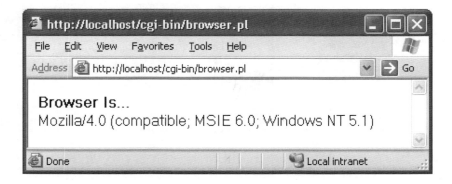

To see all the environment variables that have been set the following script loops through all the variables and writes their name and value in a HTML table:

env-vars.pl

```
#!C:\Perl\bin\perl

print "Content-type:text/html\n\n";
print "<html>";
print "<table cellspacing='1' border='1'>";

foreach $env_var (keys %ENV)
{
    print "<tr><td bgcolor='silver'>$env_var</td>";
    print "<td>$ENV{$env_var}</td></tr>";
}

print "</table>";
print "</html>";
```

A small part of the full table output is illustrated below:

See page 182 for examples of how to use the HTTP_REFERER variable.

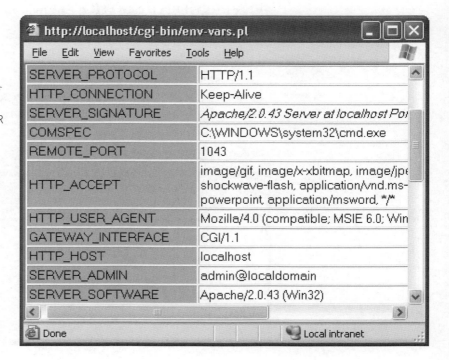

GET data from hyperlinks

In addition to simply calling PERL scripts from an HTML document hyperlinks can be used to pass information from the web browser to the PERL script on the web server.

The data to be sent to the script is appended to the URL of the PERL script as a pair with the syntax **key=value**.

This pair must be preceded by a question mark so the complete syntax looks like this:

```
protocol://domain_name/file_name?key=value
```

The other method used to send data is "POST". This is preferable to GET when submitting data from HTML forms – the "GET" method is not recommended for that purpose.

Sending data this way uses a transmission method called "GET" and this method is recorded in an environment variable called **$ENV{'REQUEST_METHOD'}**.

When the "GET" method is used the data is stored in an environment variable called **$ENV{'QUERY_STRING'}**.

The example below sends a single key/value pair to a PERL script that displays the **$ENV{'QUERY_STRING'}** and **$ENV{'REQUEST_METHOD'}** environment variables.

query.pl

```
#!C:\Perl\bin\perl

print "Content-type:text/html\n\n";
print "<html><li>Query String: $ENV{'QUERY_STRING'}";
print "<li>Method Used: $ENV{'REQUEST_METHOD'}</html>";
```

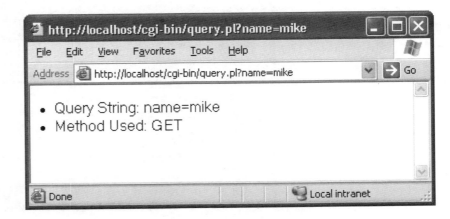

The **$ENV{'REQUEST_METHOD'}** can be tested by the PERL script to see if the "GET" method has been used to send data to the script.

The example CGI scripts on these pages are called by simply typing the URL in the browser's address bar.

If the test returns true the **$ENV{'QUERY_STRING'}** environment variable will always contain data from the browser.

The key and value are contained in the data on either side of a "=" symbol. This can be used by the PERL "split" function to assign the separate key and value to individual variables.

The following example sends a single **key=value** pair to a PERL script that tests for the "GET" method, then splits the **key=value** data around the "=" symbol.

The separated data is assigned to individual variables which are subsequently displayed in the HTML code.

split-query.pl

```perl
#!C:\Perl\bin\perl

print "Content-type:text/html\n\n";
print "<html>";

if( $ENV{"REQUEST_METHOD"} eq "GET")
{
    ($key, $value) = split(/=/, $ENV{"QUERY_STRING"} );
}

print "<li>Key Is \" $key \" ";
print "<li>Value Is \" $value \" ";
print "</html>";
```

Escape nested quotes with a preceding backslash.

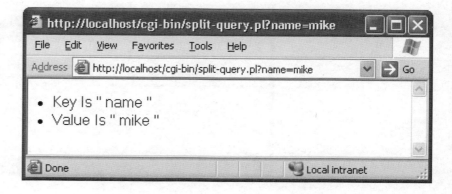

http://localhost/cgi-bin/split-query.pl?name=mike

File   Edit   View   Favorites   Tools   Help

Address   http://localhost/cgi-bin/split-query.pl?name=mike   Go

- Key Is " name "
- Value Is " mike "

Done   Local intranet

GET multiple data from links

Multiple **key=value** pairs can be sent to the web server from a hyperlink in a web browser. The **key=value** pairs must be separated by a "&" character so the syntax looks like this:

```
protocol://domain_name/file_name?key=value&key=value
```

The **$ENV{'QUERY_STRING'}** environment variable contains all the **key=value** data complete with "&" separators.

Each pair can be separated, using the "split" function around the "&" separators, and placed into an array so that each array element stores one complete **key=value** pair.

Subsequently each pair can be split into key and value data using the "split" function around the "=" character, as in this example:

split-multi.pl

```perl
#!C:\Perl\bin\perl

print "Content-type:text/html\n\n";
print "<html>";

if( $ENV{"REQUEST_METHOD"} eq "GET")
{    @pairs = split(/&/, $ENV{"QUERY_STRING"}); }

foreach $pair (@pairs)
{
    ($key, $value) = split(/=/, $pair );
    print "<li>Key: $key - Value: $value";
}

print "</html>";
```

Refer back to page 78 for more on the "foreach" loop.

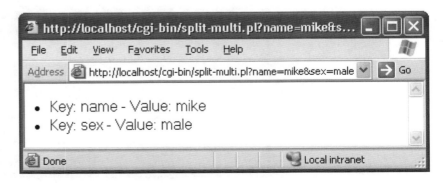

Parsing GET data

When data is sent from the browser to the server all spaces contained in the data are converted to "+" symbols. Also all non-numeric special characters are converted into their hexadecimal equivalent preceded by a "%" symbol.

For more on the translate form of pattern matching see page 106.

The receiving PERL script needs to convert both of these back into their more usual format when parsing the data.

Spaces using "+" can be translated back using this code:

```perl
$key =~ tr/+/ /;
$value =~ tr/+/ /;
```

For more on the substitute form of pattern matching see page 104. For more on the pack function see the example on page 100.

Also any special non-alphanumeric characters can be converted back from hexadecimal format to their usual format like this:

```perl
$key =~ s/%(..)/pack("c",hex($1))/eg;
$value =~ s/%(..)/pack("c",hex($1))/eg;
```

This conversion code can be added to the previous script to ensure that the data output appears correctly. The **foreach** statement in that script would now look like this:

parse-get.pl (part of)

```perl
foreach $pair (@pairs)
{
    ($key, $value) = split(/=/, $pair );
    $key =~ tr/+/ /;
    $key =~ s/%(..)/pack("c",hex($1))/eg;
    $value=~ tr/+/ /;
    $value =~ s/%(..)/pack("c",hex($1))/eg;
    print "<li>Key: $key - Value: $value";
}
```

---

http://localhost/cgi-bin/parse-get.pl?data=GET data

File   Edit   View   Favorites   Tools   Help

Address http://localhost/cgi-bin/parse-get.pl?data=GET%20data   → Go

- Key: data - Value: GET data

Done   Local intranet

POST text data from forms

A HTML form will typically be submitted to a PERL script on the server when the user pushes the form's **submit** button.

The method for transmitting the form data is specified in the HTML form as either "GET" or "POST".

When the "GET" method is used to submit the form, data is tacked onto the URL using the familiar **key=value** syntax.

However, many servers limit the amount of data that can be received by the "GET" method so it is recommended that HTML forms should always use the "POST" method.

This is how a simple HTML form might look to provide a single text field for the user to enter text and a submit button to send the text to the PERL script on the server:

post-data.html

The "action" attribute of the form element is used to specify the URL address of the PERL script that is to receive the submitted data.

```
<html>

<head>
    <title>Send Text Form</title>
</head>

<body>
<form method = "POST"
    action = "http://localhost/cgi-bin/show-text.pl">
<input type = "text" name = "text1" size = "25">
<input type = "submit" value = "Send Text">
</form>
</body>

</html>
```

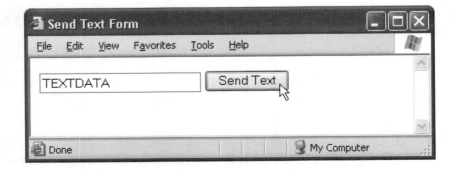

When the "POST" method is used, the environment variable **$ENV{'REQUEST_METHOD'}** is set to "POST" and the environment variable **$ENV{'CONTENT_LENGTH'}** is set to an integer value representing the data length.

The actual form data is stored at a "standard input" location on the server called "STDIN" – this can be read from a script.

PERL's "read" function can assign the form data from the "STDIN" location to a scalar variable by specifying the name of the scalar and the form data length to be assigned.

In the example below, the form data illustrated on the facing page is assigned to a scalar variable by the "read" function.

The form data is displayed in the HTML output together with both of the environment variable values.

show-text.pl

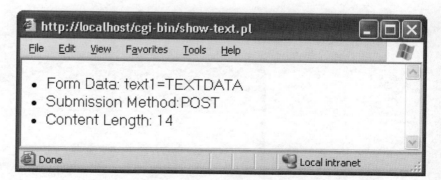

It is common practice to name the receiving scalar variable "$buffer" when reading from the "STDIN" location.

```perl
#!C:\Perl\bin\perl

print "Content-type: text/html\n\n";
print "<html>";
if( $ENV{'REQUEST_METHOD'} eq 'POST')
{
   read(STDIN, $buffer, $ENV{'CONTENT_LENGTH'});
}
print "<li>Form Data: $buffer";
print "<li>Submission Method: $ENV{'REQUEST_METHOD'}";
print "<li>Content Length: $ENV{'CONTENT_LENGTH'}";
print "</html>";
```

http://localhost/cgi-bin/show-text.pl

File   Edit   View   Favorites   Tools   Help

- Form Data: text1=TEXTDATA
- Submission Method: POST
- Content Length: 14

Done   Local intranet

POST multiple data from forms

Multiple **key=value** pairs that are submitted by a form can be split around their "&" delimiters. Each pair can then be assigned to the elements of an array. Individual keys and values can be accessed by further splitting each pair around their "=" separator as usual.

This example sends two **key=value** pairs to the PERL script which separates them and displays each component individually:

The document shown here is **post-multi.html** – it's like the **post-data.html** document on page 124 but it adds a second text input and sends its data to **show-multi.pl**.

show-multi.pl

The **key=value** pairs are handled in just the same way as seen in the GET example on page 122.

```perl
#!C:\Perl\bin\perl

print "Content-type:text/html\n\n<html>";
if( $ENV{'REQUEST_METHOD'} eq 'POST')
{
    read(STDIN, $buffer, $ENV{'CONTENT_LENGTH'});
    @pairs = split(/&/, $buffer);
}
foreach $pair (@pairs)
{
    ($key, $value) = split(/=/, $pair );
    print "<li>Key: $key - Value: $value";
}
print "</html>";
```

The value of the text2 input illustrates the conversion of spaces to "+" symbols and the ampersand character to hexadecimal.

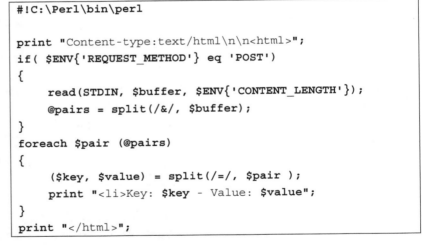

Parsing POST data

When data is sent from the browser to the server all spaces contained in the data are converted to "+" symbols. Also all non-numeric special characters are converted into their hexadecimal equivalent preceded by a "%" symbol.

The example on the opposte page illustrates these conversions.

In order to convert both of these back to their usual format the script below adds parsing routines to the previous code.

The "+" symbols spaces are now translated to spaces and regular characters are substituted for hexadecimal characters.

parse-post.pl

The translation of "+" space symbols and hexadecimal characters is handled in just the same way as the earlier GET example on page 123.

```
#!C:\Perl\bin\perl

print "Content-type:text/html\n\n<html>";
if( $ENV{'REQUEST_METHOD'} eq 'POST')
{
    read(STDIN, $buffer, $ENV{'CONTENT_LENGTH'});
    @pairs = split(/&/, $buffer);
}
foreach $pair (@pairs)
{
    ($key, $value) = split(/=/, $pair );
    $key =~ tr/+/ /;
    $value =~ tr/+/ /;
    $key =~ s/%(..)/pack("c", hex($1))/eg;
    $value =~ s/%(..)/pack("c", hex($1))/eg;
    print "<li>Key: $key - Value: $value";
}
print "</html>";
```

See page 106 for translate. See page 104 for substitute. See page 100 for the pack function.

http://localhost/cgi-bin/parse-post.pl

File   Edit   View   Favorites   Tools   Help

- Key: text1 - Value: PERL
- Key: text2 - Value: in easy steps

Done   Local intranet

The PERL form parser

Handling HTML form submissions with PERL script is so common that it is convenient to create a standard library file containing the code to carry out all the form parsing routines.

The library parser script below combines the code from previous examples in this chapter to handle both "GET" and "POST" form submission methods. It also adds a further section to allow for forms that are submitted with extra data appended to the URL.

formparser.lib

Library files have no "she-bang" line and must end with a "1". For more details on library files see page 86.

This form parser will ignore Server-Side Includes and will display a message if GET or POST methods are not used.

```perl
sub parseform
{
  if( $ENV{'REQUEST_METHOD'} eq 'GET' )
  { @pairs = split( /&/, $ENV{'QUERY_STRING'} ); }
  elsif( $ENV{'REQUEST_METHOD'} eq 'POST' )
  {
    read( STDIN, $buffer, $ENV{'CONTENT_LENGTH'} );
    @pairs = split( /&/, $buffer );
    if( $ENV{'QUERY_STRING'} )
    { @getpairs = split( /&/, $ENV{'QUERY_STRING'} );
      push( @pairs, @getpairs ); }
  }
  else
  {
    print "Content-type:text/html\n\n";
    print "Unrecognized Method - Use GET or POST.";
  }

  foreach $pair( @pairs )
  {
    ( $key, $value ) = split( /=/, $pair );
    $key =~ tr/+/ /;
    $value =~ tr/+/ /;
    $key =~ s/%(..)/pack("c", hex($1))/eg;
    $value =~ s/%(..)/pack("c", hex($1))/eg;
    $value =~ s/<!--(.|\n)*-->//g;          # ignore SSI

    if( $formdata{$key} ){$formdata{$key} .= ", $value";}
    else{ $formdata{$key} = $value; }
  }
}

1;
```

The form parser creates a hash called **%formdata** in which all the parsed keys and their values are stored. Multiple values for the same key are stored as a comma-delimited list.

In order for the library file to be accessible to PERL scripts it must be placed in Apache's **cgi-bin** directory.

The example below uses the form parser to process the illustrated HTML form and displays the input values:

*The HTML document shown here is named **post-colors.html**. – it has 3 text inputs named **color1**, **color2** and **color3**.*

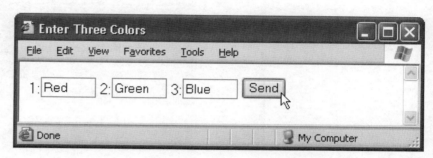

show-colors.pl

```
#!C:\Perl\bin\perl

require "formparser.lib";
&parseform;

print "Content-type:text/html\n\n<html>";
print "You entered these colors: ";
print "$formdata{'color1'}, ";
print "$formdata{'color2'} and ";
print "$formdata{'color3'} </html>";
```

*The form parser **formparser.lib** is associated with the PERL script using the "require" keyword. The parseform subroutine is called by the "&parseform;" instruction.*

Output all parsed form data

This example loops through the **%formdata** hash, created by the form parser, to show all the parsed keys and values:

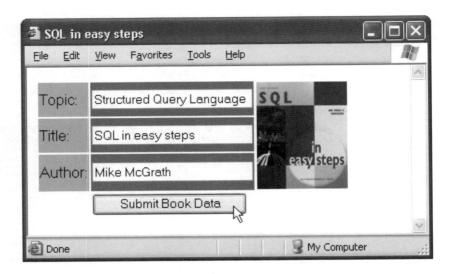

show-all.pl

```
#!C:\Perl\bin\perl

require "formparser.lib";
&parseform;

print "Content-type: text/html\n\n<html>";

foreach $key (keys %formdata)
{    print "<li>Key: $key - Value: $formdata{$key}"; }

print "</html>";
```

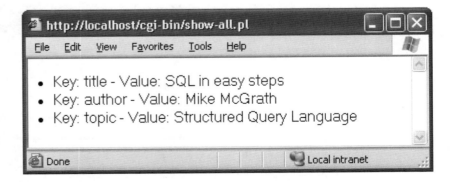

Working with files

This chapter illustrates how PERL scripts can read and write text files on the server. Examples demonstrate how these features can create a simple hit counter and guest book.

Covers

Chapter Eleven

Reading a text file

The PERL "open" and "close" functions are used to both read from, and write to, text files on the server.

The "open" function creates a "text stream" containing the contents of the first line of characters in the text file.

Remember to close the text stream after assigning the contents.

A "file handle" label must be given, as the first argument to the "open" function – this can then be used to refer to the text stream.

The second argument specifies the name of the text file to be opened. If the text file is not in the **cgi-bin** directory the full path to the text file should be stated.

A "<" character must immediately precede the file name or path to indicate that the text file is to be read.

This example opens a text file in the **cgi-bin** directory then assigns the first line to a scalar for subsequent display in the output.

textfile.txt

```
Then join in hand brave Americans all
By uniting we stand, by dividing we fall.
- John Dickinson 1732 - 1808
```

opentext.pl

```perl
#!/usr/bin/perl

open(TXT, "<textfile.txt");    # open the text file
$text = <TXT>;                 # assign its contents
close(TXT);                    # close the text file

print "Content-type:text/html\n\n <html>";
print "Text File Contents:<br/>$text  </html>";
```

Notice the syntax used with the label when assigning to a text stream – the file handle label must be enclosed in angle brackets.

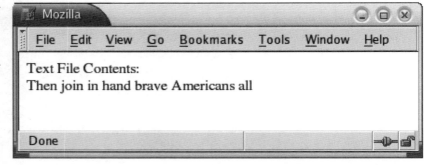

A text stream from an opened text file can store multiple lines of text when assigned to an array variable. Each array element contains one line of characters from the text file.

The example below uses the relative address of the text file placed in Apache's "logs" folder to open the text stream.

All lines in the text stream are assigned to an array using the file handle label.

The "foreach" loop displays each line of text contained in the array elements when writing the HTML output.

textfile.txt

```
Then join in hand brave Americans all
By uniting we stand, by dividing we fall.
- John Dickinson 1732 - 1808
```

alltext.pl

```perl
#!/usr/bin/perl

open(TXT, "<textfile.txt");
@text = <TXT>;
close(TXT);
print "Content-type:text/html\n\n <html>";
print "Text File Contents:<br/>";
foreach $line(@text)
{
   print "$line <br/>";
}
print "</html>";
```

Remember to close the text stream after assigning the contents.

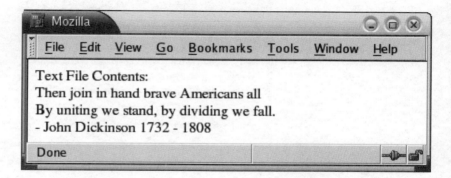

Writing to a text file

The PERL "open" function can be used to create a new text file or update an existing file by overwriting its contents.

First the PERL "open" function opens the existing text file or, if none exists, creates a new file with the specified name.

The "open" function takes two arguments to specify a file handle label for the text stream and the name of the text file.

A ">" character must immediately precede the file name to indicate that the function should write to the file.

*Always place text files in the **cgi-bin** folder to avoid confusion.*

The "print" function states the name of the file handle then the string to be written in the text file.

This can be repeated to add more content before the text stream is closed by the "close" function.

Here a new text file called "datafile.txt" is created then two lines of text are added before the text stream is closed:

writetext.pl

```perl
#!/usr/bin/perl

print "Content-type:text/html\n\n";

# write to a new or existing text file
open(TXT, ">datafile.txt");
print TXT "Message From CGI Script:\n";
print TXT "File handling is easy with Perl";
close(TXT);
```

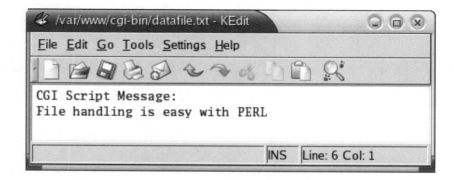

Hit counter

A text file on the server can be used as a "hit-counter" that stores an integer value recording the number of times a web page has been opened.

For more on formatting see the examples on page 92–93.

This example reads the current count, then increments that value and saves the new count back in the text file. The new count is formatted to 5 digits then displayed in the output.

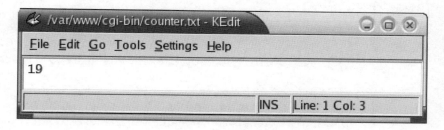

counter.pl

Remember that the file permissions on Linux systems must be set to allow text files to be read from and written to – PERL files must also be set to executable.

```perl
#!/usr/bin/perl

# get the last count value (currently it's 19)
open(COUNT, "<counter.txt");
$num = <COUNT>;
close(COUNT);

$num++;    # increment the count value by 1 (up to 20)

# save the new count value (it's now 20)
open(COUNT, ">counter.txt");
print COUNT $num;
close(COUNT);

$num = sprintf("%05d",$num);    # format count (00020)

print "Content-type:text/html\n\n";
print "<html>You are visitor number $num</html>";
```

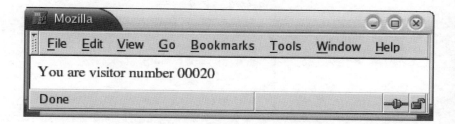

Appending to a text file

The PERL "open" function can be used to add text to an existing text file by appending text to its current contents. First the PERL "open" function opens the existing text file that is to be updated, or it creates a new file if none already exists. The "open" function takes two arguments to specify a file handle label for the text stream and the name of the text file.

Text will be appended immediately following any existing text. Use "\n" to state new lines.

The ">>" characters must immediately precede the file name to indicate that the function should append text.

The "print" function states the name of the file handle then the string to be appended to the text file. This can be repeated before the text stream is closed by the "close" function.

Here an existing text file called "content.txt" is opened then more text is appended before the text stream is closed:

appendtext.pl

```
#!/usr/bin/perl

print "Content-type:text/html\n\n";
open(TXT, ">>content.txt");
print TXT " and \nhere is some more text.";
print TXT "\n - PERL appended this extra text.";
close(TXT);
```

Guest messages

A simple guest book appends messages from a form to a text file which can then be read to display all the messages:

This form has two text inputs named "msg" and "from" whose names and values are submitted to the script as **key=value** pairs.

msg.pl

A form parser processes the submitted data which is then appended to a text file, as in the example on the previous page. All the text file content is then assigned to an array, as with the example on page 133.

```perl
#!/usr/bin/perl

require "formparser.lib"; &parseform;

$txt = $formdata{'msg'};
$name = $formdata{'from'};

open( TXT, ">>messages.txt" );
print TXT "Message: $txt - From $name \n";
close(TXT);

open( DATA, "<messages.txt" );
@data = < DATA >;
close( DATA );

print "Content-type:text/html\n\n";
foreach $item(@data){ print "<li>$item"; }
print "</html>";
```

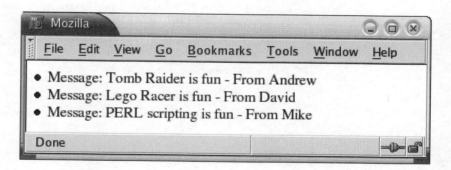

Exclusive file access

When a text file has been opened by a script to read, write or append data, it is essential (to avoid file errors) that no other script attempts to access that same text file concurrently.

The PERL "flock" function performs a "file lock" to ensure that the operation being performed on the text file will not be interrupted.

The "flock" function takes two arguments to specify the file handle label and a numeric indicator of the type of lock required. An indicator of "2" signifies that exclusive access should be granted to that instance of the script.

When creating PERL scripts on a platform not supporting "flock" include any flock calls in the script but comment them out with a "#" until the script is ready to be uploaded to the server.

On completion of the operation with the text file, the script should again call the "flock" function to release the file for access by other scripts. The releasing call must state the file handle label and an indicator of "8" as its two arguments.

This script uses the "flock" function when appending a date string to an existing text file:

file-lock.pl

```perl
#!/usr/bin/perl

print "Content-type:text/html\n\n";

$gmt = gmtime(time);
open(NOW, ">datefile.txt");
flock(NOW, 2);                    # lock the file
print NOW $gmt;
flock(NOW, 8);                    # unlock the file
close(NOW);
```

To limit the length of time that the text file is inaccessible to other scripts, only operations directly involving the text file should be performed while the file is locked.

For instance, in the example above, the date is assigned to the variable before the file is locked.

The PERL "flock" function is supported on Linux and Windows XP platforms – it may not perform correctly on other platforms.

Adding error messages

In the event that the anticipated file operation fails, it is good to advise the user of the error. When an error occurs PERL sets the special variable "$!" with a string describing that error.

A subroutine can be used to write the error message contained in the "$!" variable when an error occurs. The PERL "exit" function stops any further execution of the script code after the error message has been written.

In the example below the script attempts to open a text file. When the file is not found the error message contained in "$!" is passed to the subroutine, for display to the user, and the script gets halted.

error.pl

See page 84 for more on passing values to subroutines with "$_[0]".

```perl
#!/usr/bin/perl

open( TXT, "<nonsuch.txt") || &error($!);
@data = < TXT >;
close( TXT );

print "Content-type:text/html\n\n <html>";
foreach $item(@data)
{
    print "<li> $item";
}

print "</html>";

sub error
{
    print "Content-type:text/html\n\n";
    print "<html><h3>Error: $_[0] </h3></html>";
    exit;
}
```

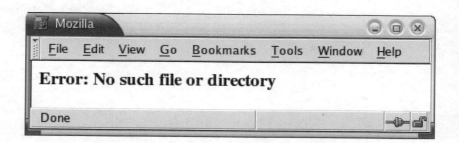

Renaming files

The PERL "rename" function is useful to rename files and also to relocate files into other folders. It requires two arguments to specify the old and new file names. If the file is not in the **cgi-bin** directory the absolute address is needed.

In the example below one file is simply renamed from **data.txt** to **newdata.txt**. A second file is renamed from **log.txt** to **newlog.txt** and simultaneously relocated to the **logs** sub-folder. A third file named **temp.txt** is simply relocated to the **logs** sub-folder.

The file URLs specified as the "rename" function arguments must be contained in quotes.

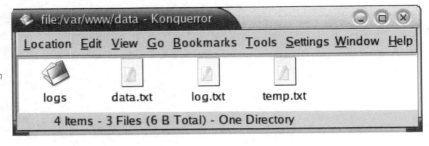

rename.pl

```perl
#!/usr/bin/perl

print "Content-type:text/html\n\n";

rename("/var/www/data/data.txt",
        "/var/www/data/newdata.txt");
rename("/var/www/data/log.txt",
        "/var/www/data/logs/newlog.txt");
rename("/var/www/data/temp.txt",
        "/var/www/data/logs/temp.txt");
```

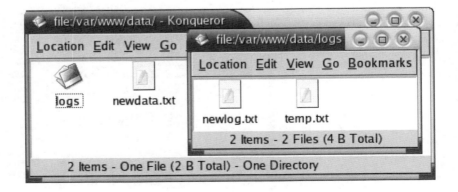

Deleting files

Files can be deleted from the server directories from within CGI scripts by utilizing the PERL "unlink" function. The "unlink" function takes the name of the file to delete as its sole argument.

If the file is not in the **cgi-bin** directory the absolute address is needed.

Multiple files to be deleted can be specified as a comma-delimited list forming the single argument to the function.

The following example builds on the example on the previous example to remove both files from the **logs** sub-folder.

unlink.pl

```perl
#!/usr/bin/perl

print "Content-type:text/html\n\n";

unlink("/var/www/data/logs/newlog.txt");
unlink("/var/www/data/logs/temp.txt");
```

For details on how to delete the empty folder in this example see the "rmdir" function that is demonstrated on page 147.

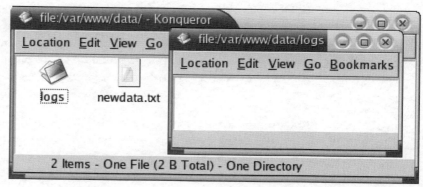

To verify that the files no longer exist the script could test their file status using the "-e" PERL operator. This is part of a range of special operators that are described and demonstrated on the next page.

File status

A file can be set with permissions to determine how it may be used. For instance, a file that is "read-only" does not permit PERL to write new content to it. The status of a file and its permissions can be tested with the special PERL operators listed in this table:

For more on file permissions see page 148.

Operator	Operation
-e	Does the file exist?
-d	Is the file a directory?
-r	Do the permissions allow the file to be read?
-w	Do the permissions allow writing to the file?
-x	Do the permissions allow the file to be executed?

status.pl

This example checks the status of the newdata.txt file from the previous page.

```perl
#!/usr/bin/perl

$file = "/var/www/data/newdata.txt";
$e = (-e $file) ? "exists" : "absent";
$d = (-d $file) ? "directory" : "non-directory";
$r = (-r $file) ? "readable" : "non-readable";
$w = (-w $file) ? "writable" : "non-writable";
$x = (-x $file) ? "executable" : "non-executable";

print "Content-type:text/html\n\n";
print "<html><table border='1' width='100%'>";
print "<tr><th>Status of $file :</th></tr>";
print "<tr><td>$e, $d, $r, $w, $x</td></tr>";
print "</table></html>";
```

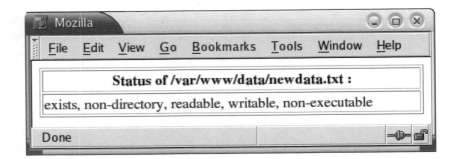

Handling directories

This chapter illustrates how to work with files and directory structures. It is especially useful for Windows users who are unfamiliar with permission settings on Unix-based systems. The text explains the importance of file permissions and the examples demonstrate how to set them with PERL.

Covers

Chapter Twelve

View the working directory

The contents of a directory can be viewed in a similar manner to that used to read text files.

PERL's "opendir" function requires a file handle label and directory address to open the directory to be viewed.

The contents can be assigned to an array by the "readdir" function that specifies the file handle label as its argument.

Finally the directory text stream must be closed with the PERL "closedir" function and the file handle label.

This example views all files in the working **cgi-bin** directory and sorts them into alphabetical order:

view-dir.pl

```perl
#!/usr/bin/perl

opendir(DIR, ".");
@files = readdir(DIR);
@files = sort(@files);
closedir(DIR);

print "Content-type:text/html\n\n<html>";
foreach $file(@files)
{
    print "$file - ";
}
print "</html>";
```

The current directory is addressed by "." while ".." addresses the next directory level up.

Notice that the contents of the directory that is viewed includes all system files.

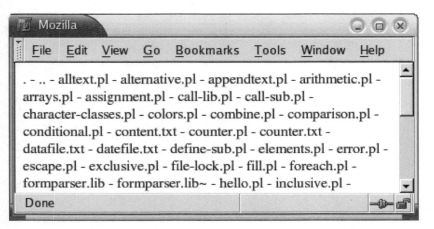

```
Mozilla
File  Edit  View  Go  Bookmarks  Tools  Window  Help

. - .. - alltext.pl - alternative.pl - appendtext.pl - arithmetic.pl -
arrays.pl - assignment.pl - call-lib.pl - call-sub.pl -
character-classes.pl - colors.pl - combine.pl - comparison.pl -
conditional.pl - content.txt - counter.pl - counter.txt -
datafile.txt - datefile.txt - define-sub.pl - elements.pl - error.pl -
escape.pl - exclusive.pl - file-lock.pl - fill.pl - foreach.pl -
formparser.lib - formparser.lib~ - hello.pl - inclusive.pl -
Done
```

View a selected file type

The PERL "grep" function can be used to restrict the files listed in a directory view to just one specific file type.

Two arguments are needed by the "grep" function.

The first argument specifies a pattern that is the file type and the second argument provides a full list of directory files.

Only when the "grep" function matches its search pattern, in the list of files, is that file assigned to an array element.

The example below searches for a match to the string ".txt" and assigns only correct matches to the files array:

view-file.pl

Use a backslash to escape the "." period character in the search pattern.

```perl
#!/usr/bin/perl

opendir(DIR, ".");

@files = grep( /\.txt/, readdir(DIR) );
@files = sort(@files);
closedir(DIR);

print "Content-type:text/html\n\n<html>";
foreach $file(@files)
{
    print "<li>$file";
}
print "</html>";
```

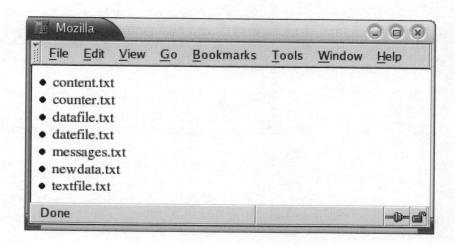

Creating and deleting directories

PERL can create new directories on the server using the "mkdir" function with two arguments.

The first argument specifies the name and address of the new directory folder.

The second argument sets the permissions code for the new directory that control how the folder can be accessed.

Typically the widest range of permissions are set with the code "0755" to permit read and execute operations.

The example below creates a new folder, called **refs**, with read and execute permissions in the Apache directory structure:

mkdir.pl

```perl
#!/usr/bin/perl

print "Content-type:text/html\n\n";

mkdir("../refs", 0755);
```

For more on permissions see page 148.

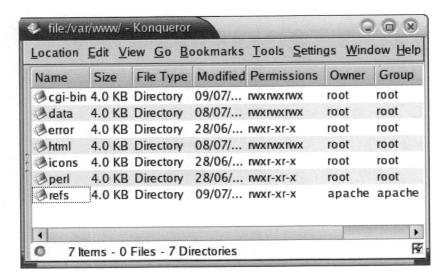

Notice that the "owner" of the new **refs** directory is stated as Apache, rather than a user by name. Technically a directory that has been created from a PERL script has the script itself as its owner.

Empty directories can be removed with the "rmdir" function that takes a single argument to specify the directory address.

An attempt to delete a directory that is not empty will fail – as seen in the example below. Here the **refs** directory contains a single file called **page.txt**.

rmdir-1.pl

```
#!/usr/bin/perl

print "Content-type:text/html\n\n";
rmdir("../refs")|| &error($!);

sub error
{
    print "<html>Error: $_[0] </html>"; exit;
}
```

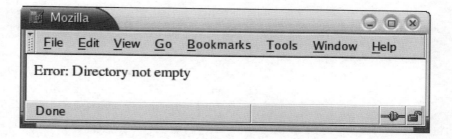

To delete the directory the modified script below checks for the existence of the file called **page.txt** and removes it. Now that the directory is empty it can also be deleted.

rmdir-2.pl

The special "-e" operator is used to check file status – See page 142.

```
#!/usr/bin/perl

print "Content-type:text/html\n\n";
$file="../refs/page.txt";
if(-e $file){ unlink($file) }

rmdir("../refs") || die &error($!);

sub error
{
    print "<html>Error: $_[0] </html>"; exit;
}
```

Permission values

Directories and files have an inherent set of permissions that control how they may be accessed for reading, writing and executing operations.

The permissions are given numeric values denoting if they can be read (4), write (2) and execute(1).

These may be combined by adding the numeric values. For instance, a file with read (4) and write (2) permissions, but not execute permission, would have a total value 6 (4 + 2).

Permission values are given in this way to the three types of user who may access the directory or file in the strict order of "owner", "group" and "public".

The file's "owner" is generally the creator of the file who would typically want full read, write and execute permissions.

The "group" permissions relate only to user groups on Unix-based systems so can usually be given the same permissions as those given to the "public" category.

Typically, a file would have permissions giving full unlimited access to the "owner" and permissions to read and execute to "group" and "public" – a value setting of 755.

In PERL the permissions code always requires a leading zero, so the permissions code for this directory becomes 0755.

The table below lists commonly used permission settings showing how they affect each type of user with abbreviations of "r" for read, "w" for write and "x" for execute.

For setting permissions on the Unix server see page 181.

File Type	Permissions	Owner	Group	Public
Directory	0777	rwx	rwx	rwx
Executables eg. PERL scripts	0755	rwx	r-x	r-x
Non-executables eg. Text files	0644	rw-	r--	r--

Changing permissions

A script must have full directory permissions (7) to allow it to create, delete or rename files within that directory. Permissions of directories and files can be changed by PERL scripts using the "chmod" function.

The "chmod" function takes two arguments to specify the permission code values and the address of the directory or file whose permissions are to be changed.

The example below tests for the existence of a directory before changing its permissions and writing a confirmation. If the directory is not found the alternative message is displayed. If an error occurs the subroutine displays a helpful error message.

chmod.pl

```perl
#!/usr/bin/perl

print "Content-type:text/html\n\n <html>";
if(-e "../refs")
{
    chmod(0777, "../refs") || &error($!);
    print "Refs directory permissions set to 0777";
}
else
{
    print "Refs directory was not found<br/>";
    print " - No permissions have changed.";
}
print "</html>";

sub error
{
    print "Error: $_[0] </html>"; exit;
}
```

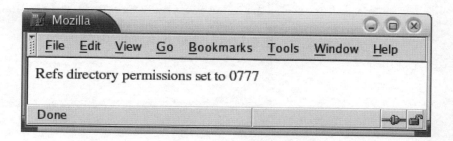

Change the working directory

The "working" directory is normally the one containing the PERL script and is usually the **cgi-bin** directory on the server.

Other directories and files within the "working" directory can be addressed simply by their file name.

Directories and files outside the "working" directory must be referenced by their absolute address.

The PERL "chdir" function can specify any directory as the working directory so its files can then be addressed just by file name. This is convenient where a script uses several files contained in another directory.

This example makes a directory called **refs** into the working directory. You can then address its files just by their names, without needing to state any path:

chdir.pl

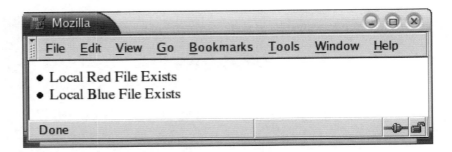

The terminating semi-colon may be omitted after the final statement in a statement block — as seen here.

```perl
#!/usr/bin/perl

print "Content-type:text/html\n\n<html>";

chdir("../refs") || &error($!);

if(-e "red.txt") { print "<li>Local Red File Exists" }
if(-e "blue.txt"){ print "<li>Local Blue File Exists" }
print "</html>";

sub error
{
    print "Error:$_[0] </html>"; exit;
}
```

Data persistence

This chapter illustrates how user data can be retained as the user browses across different web pages. There are demonstrations of how to store data in hidden forms, in server files and in browser cookies. Also examples demonstrate how access to cookie information can be restricted.

Covers

Chapter Thirteen

Storing data in hidden form fields

A HTML form may contain hidden input fields that can be used to great effect by PERL scripts to store data.

A script that writes a HTML document can include some hidden form fields and assign stored data as their values. In this way the hidden form fields can retain stored data as the user moves from page to page.

The example illustrating this in action starts with a simple HTML document containing a form with just two text inputs.

When the user submits this form to the server the PERL script extracts the entered values and assigns them to scalar variables. The HTML page created by this script writes these scalar values as hidden form values stored in the new HTML form. When that second HTML form is submitted the next script extracts all form values – including those in the hidden fields.

Finally the script generates a HTML document that displays the data entered by the user in both previous HTML forms.

order.html

```
<html>
<head> <title>Order Items</title> </head>
<body>
<form method = "POST"
    action = "http://localhost/cgi-bin/order.pl">
Item required: <input type="text" name="itm" size="15"/>
<br/>Quantity: <input type="text" name="qty" size="3" />
<input type = "submit" value = "Submit Items" />
</form> </body> </html>
```

Keep the same name for data inputs to make the movement easier to follow.

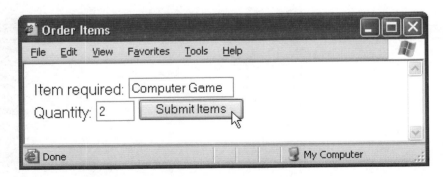

order.pl

```perl
#!C:\Perl\bin\perl

require "formparser.lib"; &parseform;

print << "DOC";
Content-type:text/html\n\n <html>
<form method = "POST"
     action = "http://localhost/cgi-bin/final.pl">
Name: <input type = "text" name = "name" size = "15"/>
<input type = "submit" value = "Submit" />
<input type="hidden" name="itm" value="$formdata{itm}" />
<input type="hidden" name="qty" value="$formdata{qty}" />
</form> </html>
DOC
```

final.pl

This script adds an "s" to the end of the item for multiple-quantity orders.

```perl
#!C:\Perl\bin\perl

require "formparser.lib"; &parseform;

print "Content-type:text/html\n\n<html>";
print "$formdata{name} has ordered ";
print "$formdata{qty} $formdata{itm}";
if($formdata{qty} > 1){ print "s" };
print "</html>";
```

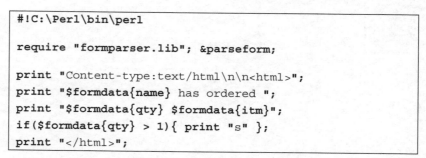

Storing data in text files

Data that has been entered by the user can be stored on the server in a text file so will not be lost as the user navigates around different pages.

The stored data can be retrieved for use in the generation of a new page at any time.

The following example is similar to the previous one but now stores user input in a text file.

First the user enters data into a simple HTML form:

goods.html

```
<html> <head> <title>Order Items</title> </head> <body>
<form method = "POST"
    action = "http://localhost/cgi-bin/goods.pl">
Item required: <input type="text" name="itm" size="15" />
<br/>Quantity: <input type="text" name="qty" size="3" />
<input type="submit" value="Submit Items" />
</form> </body> </html>
```

Add commas between saved data items so they can be split into parts later.

The form values are then extracted and saved in a text file:

goods.pl (part of)

```
#!C:\Perl\bin\perl

require "formparser.lib"; &parseform;

open(SAVE,  ">save.txt");
print SAVE "$formdata{itm},$formdata{qty}";
close(SAVE);

print << "DOC";
```

goods.pl
(cont'd)

```
Content-type:text/html\n\n <html>
<form method = "POST"
     action = "http://localhost/cgi-bin/summary.pl" >
Name: <input type="text" name="name" size="15" />
<input type="submit" value="Submit" /> </form> </html>
DOC
```

Finally the stored data is retrieved for display:

summary.pl

For more on reading text from files see page 132.

```
#!C:\Perl\bin\perl

require "formparser.lib"; &parseform;

open(SAVE, "<save.txt");
$list = <SAVE>;
close(SAVE);
@data = split( /,/ , $list);

print "Content-type:text/html\n\n<html>";
print "$formdata{name} ordered $data[1] $data[0]";
if($data[1] > 1){ print "s" };
print "</html>";
```

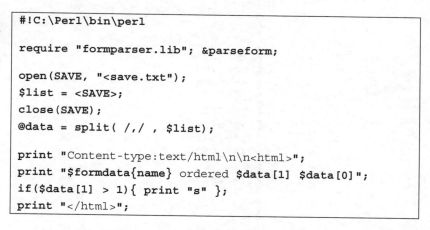

Internet Explorer cookies

A cookie file can be used to store data on a user's computer in text format up to a limit of around 4000 characters.

The user's computer can store up to 20 cookies from a single site and a maximum of 300 cookies in total.

On the Windows XP platform Internet Explorer saves the cookie files in a folder at **C:\Documents and Settings\[user]\Cookies** where the actual user name is substituted for *[user]*.

The cookie file shown below contains two cookies that each start with the name and value of that cookie.

This is followed by the domain and path address of the document for which this cookie applies.

The list of numbers at the end of each cookie are just used by the local system to store the data.

Documents and Settings
- All Users
- Default User
- Mike McGrath
  - Application Data
  - Cookies
  - Debug
  - Desktop
  - Favorites

This cookie file contains the cookies for the example on page 162.

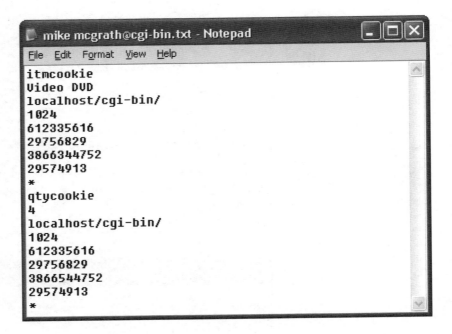

```
mike mcgrath@cgi-bin.txt - Notepad
File  Edit  Format  View  Help

itmcookie
Video DVD
localhost/cgi-bin/
1024
612335616
29756829
3866344752
29574913
*
qtycookie
4
localhost/cgi-bin/
1024
612335616
29756829
3866544752
29574913
*
```

Netscape cookies

On the Windows XP platform Netscape browsers store cookie data in a file called "cookies.txt". This is typically buried deep at the location **C:\Documents and Settings** *[user]***\Application Data\Mozilla\Profiles***[user]******[obscure-number]***\cookies.txt**. Again, the actual user name should be substituted for *[user]*.

It is interesting to see where, and how, cookie data is stored – but, thankfully the methods for storage and retrieval remains the same, irrespective of the browser.

The cookies contain the domain and path details together with a numeric representation of the cookie expiry date. The cookie name and value is given at the end of each cookie.

The cookie file below shows the Netscape equivalent of the Internet Explorer cookie file on the opposite page:

For more on cookie expiry dates see the example on page 160.

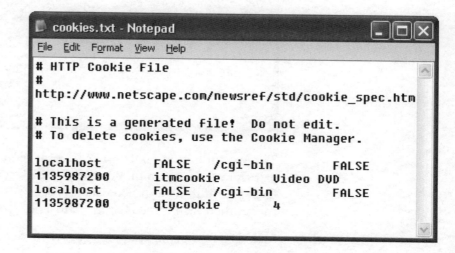

Storing data in cookies

Form data can be stored in a cookie file so that another web page in that site can retrieve the data to use again. Typically this creates a "shopping cart" arrangement where the user can add chosen items for totalling later. Each item is stored in a cookie then all items can be finally retrieved for display on a summary page.

The first step is to send data for an order item from the web page to the PERL script that will add the data to a cookie file.

The HTML document shown below produces a form in which the user has specified an item to order, and stated a required quantity:

remit.html

```html
<html>
<head> <title>Order Items</title> </head>
<body>
<form method = "POST"
    action = "http://localhost/cgi-bin/set-cookie.pl">
Item required: <input type="text" name="wot" size="15" />
Quantity: <input type="text" name="num" size="3"/>
<input type="submit" value="Send"/>
</form>
</body>
</html>
```

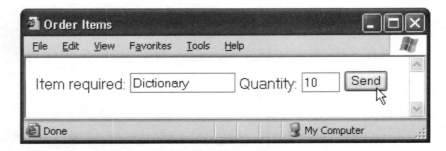

The submit button on the HTML form sends the **name=value** pair from the form to the set-cookie PERL script listed opposite. Each part of this submitted data is processed as normal by the form parser, then each value is assigned to a new cookie.

Making a new cookie requires the syntax **Set-Cookie:** followed immediately by a given name to identify the data. The given names in the example are "wotcookie" and "numcookie".

In this example "wotcookie" stores the description of the item and "numcookie" stores the required quantity.

When the set-cookie script is executed, the PERL environment variable header **$ENV{'HTTP_COOKIE'}** already contains details of existing cookies. The submitted values now get stored in memory on the server and are available from the **$ENV{'HTTP_COOKIE'} environment** variable in subsequent web pages in this session. The header details are received before the cookies are set, so the script cannot update the cookies first.

Do not leave any space between the "Set-Cookie:" syntax and the given name of the cookie.

The script below reveals details of any previously set cookies then sets the new cookie values for use in subsequent pages.

set-cookie.pl

```
#!C:\Perl\bin\perl

require "formparser.lib"; &parseform;

print "Set-Cookie:wotcookie = $formdata{'wot'} \n";
print "Set-Cookie:numcookie = $formdata{'num'} \n";

print "Content-type:text/html\n\n<html>";
if($ENV{'HTTP_COOKIE'}){ print "$ENV{'HTTP_COOKIE'}" }
else{ print "No cookies previously set." }
print "</html>";
```

Note that this example will print a default message if no cookies are found.

The script above could also write a link to a subsequent PERL script to display the current cookies stored in the server memory.

When the browser is closed the session ends and the cookie values are lost because the set-cookie script does not specify an expiry date for that cookie data – cookies are only written to the cookie file if a future expiry date is correctly specified.

Cookie life span

Unless an expiry date is specified when creating a cookie the life of that cookie is limited to the current browser session. In this situation the cookie data is only stored in the computer RAM memory and a cookie file is not written. So when the browser application is terminated this transient cookie data is lost.

Setting an expiry date causes a cookie file to be written into the appropriate folder location. This means that the cookie data can be accessed over and over – until its specified expiry date.

Re-setting the expiry date to a date before the present date will delete the cookie permanently.

To set an expiry date requires that the cookie's "expires" attribute be assigned a final date in a particular date format. The date format should start with the 3-letter abbreviation for the weekday followed by a comma. Next the date is stated in the format DD-MMM-YYYY where DD is a 2-digit day number of the month, MMM is a 3-letter abbreviation of a month and YYYY is a 4-digit year. Then the time is stated in the format HH:MM:SS where HH is a 2-digit hour of a 24-hour clock, MM is a 2-digit number of minutes and SS is a 2-digit number of seconds. Finally the time format is specified as Greenwich Mean Time using "GMT".

This example creates a cookie to expire at the end of 2005. The data is written in the cookie file and saved when the session ends.

save-cookie.pl

```
#!C:\Perl\bin\perl

print "Set-Cookie:wotcookie = submitted-data;
        expires=Sat, 31-Dec-2005 00:00:00 GMT\n";
print "Content-type:text/html\n\n";
```

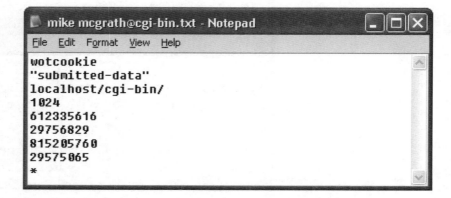

Restricting access

When a cookie is created the current domain and path are assigned automatically to its "domain" and "path" attributes.

Only PERL scripts in that domain and on that path will be permitted to read the cookie data.

The cookie's "domain" attribute may only be assigned the domain from which the cookie is set, to ensure that PERL scripts on other domains cannot access that cookie.

Access to the cookie can be restricted to PERL scripts contained on a specific path by explicitly setting the "path" attribute.

Here, a PERL script in the **cgi-bin** directory sets a cookie that can only be accessed by PERL scripts in the **cgi-bin/sub** sub-directory in the same domain:

write-cookie.pl

```
#!C:\Perl\bin\perl
require "formparser.lib"; &parseform;

print "Set-Cookie:namecookie=$formdata{'name'};
          expires=Sat,31-Dec-2005 00:00:00 GMT;
          path=/cgi-bin/sub; \n";
print "Content-type:text/html\n\n";
```

This cookie could be set from a hyperlink, such as

`http://localhost/cgi-bin/write-cookie.pl?name=PERL fun`.

Only scripts in the sub-folder **cgi-bin/sub** can access this cookie.

Scripts in the "cgi-bin" directory cannot access the cookie created in this example.

```
mike mcgrath@sub.txt - Notepad
File  Edit  Format  View  Help
namecookie
Perl fun
localhost/cgi-bin/sub
1024
612335616
29756829
683743872
29575068
*
```

Using cookie data

Retrieving data from the cookie file requires that the pieces of cookie data must be split into their separate components. Each cookie is automatically separated by a semi-colon and a space when it is saved in the cookie file.

This can be used to split the cookies into an array where each element contains one **name=value** cookie pair.

The data in the cookie file is accessed via the environment variable
$ENV{'HTTP_COOKIE'}.

Each of these pairs can then be split around the "=" symbol into separate hashes – to make the **name=value** data accessible.

This example first creates two cookies to store user input from a HTML form, then writes a second form:

products.html
(not listed)

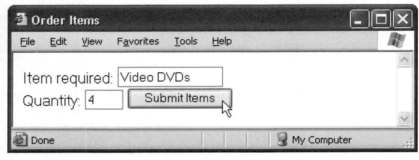

products.pl

```
#!C:\Perl\bin\perl

require "formparser.lib"; &parseform;

print "Set-Cookie:item-cookie = $formdata{'itm'};
    expires = Sat,31-Dec-2005 00:00:00 GMT\n";
print "Set-Cookie:qty-cookie = $formdata{'qty'};
    expires = Sat,31-Dec-2005 00:00:00 GMT\n";

print << "DOC";
Content-type:text/html\n\n <html>
<form method="POST"
    action="http://localhost/cgi-bin/report.pl" >
Name: <input type="text" name="name" size="15"/>
<input type="submit" value="Submit" />
</form> </html>

DOC
```

The values from the example HTML form inputs named "itm" and "qty" are stored in cookies named "item-cookie" and "qty-cookie".

When the second form is submitted, the PERL script below splits the cookies into an array called "@cookies", then splits each pair into a hash called "%data". The script finally writes a HTML page that uses both the data retrieved from the cookies and user input from the second form:

report.pl

The original HTML form input values are now accessible from the "%data" hash by specifying the cookie name as the key.

```perl
#!C:\Perl\bin\perl

require "formparser.lib"; &parseform;

if( $ENV{'HTTP_COOKIE'} )
{
    @cookies=split( /; /,$ENV{'HTTP_COOKIE'} );
    foreach $cookie (@cookies)
    {    ( $name, $value ) = split( /=/, $cookie );
         $data{ $name } = $value; }
}

print "Content-type:text/html\n\n<html>";
print "$formdata{name} ordered ";
print "$data{'qty-cookie'} $data{'item-cookie'}";
if($data{'qty-cookie'} > 1){ print "s" };
print "</html>";
```

Refused cookie message

If the user has selected browser settings to disallow cookies, it is worthwhile providing a message to explain that the cookie data required by a script cannot be found.

The example below adds an alternative subroutine to the script on the previous page that will write a message if the $ENV{'HTTP_COOKIE'} variable is empty.

refuse.pl

```perl
#!C:\Perl\bin\perl

require "formparser.lib"; &parseform;

if($ENV{'HTTP_COOKIE'})
{ @cookies=split(/; /,$ENV{'HTTP_COOKIE'});
  foreach $cookie(@cookies)
 {($name,$value)=split(/=/,$cookie);$data{$name}=$value}
} else { &notice }

print "Content-type:text/html\n\n<html>";
print "$formdata{name} ordered ";
print "$data{'qty-cookie'} $data{'item-cookie'}";
if($data{'qty-cookie'} > 1){ print "s" };
print "</html>";

sub notice
{
  print "Content-type:text/html\n\n<html>";
  print "<b>The browser cannot locate data!</b><hr/>";
  print "Please enable cookies in your browser.</html>";
  exit;
}
```

It is very safe to allow cookies on a computer but some users are still wary.

Form inputs

This chapter demonstrates how PERL scripts can use different types of HTML form input from checkboxes, radio buttons and option menus. Also, examples show how PERL can navigate between web pages and send email. A survey application is included to illustrate several of these features in action together.

Covers

Chapter Fourteen

Checkboxes

Checkboxes are used to allow users to select items in a HTML form. Each checkbox must have a unique name assigned to its "name" attribute in the HTML code.

Also, each check box "value" attribute should be assigned a value to be associated with that box.

The following example illustrates a HTML form containing a list of check boxes.

When the form is submitted, the **name=value** pairs of any boxes which are checked, are processed by the form parser. All the selected values are then displayed in the generated HTML output.

chkbox.html

When a form is submitted only the *name=value* pair of any checked checkboxes will be sent to the server – those that remain unchecked are ignored.

```
<html> <head> <title>Check Boxes</title> </head> <body>

<form method = "POST"
     action = "http://localhost/cgi-bin/chkbox.pl">

<b>Select 3 Favorite Destinations: </b><br/>
<input type="checkbox" name="NY" value="New York" />
New York <br/>
<input type="checkbox" name="SF" value="San Francisco" />
San Francisco <br/>
<input type="checkbox" name="TY" value="Tokyo" />
Tokyo <br/>
<input type="checkbox" name="SY" value="Sydney" />
Sydney <br/>
<input type="checkbox" name="CT" value="Cape Town" />
Cape Town <br/>
<input type="checkbox" name="AT" value="Athens" />
Athens <br/>
<input type="checkbox" name="MO" value="Moscow" />
Moscow <br/>
<input type="checkbox" name="PA" value="Paris" />
Paris <br/>
<input type="checkbox" name="LO" value="London" />
London <br/>
<input type="submit" value="Submit Selections" />
</form>
</body>
</html>
```

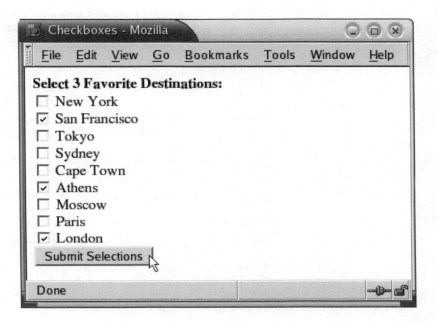

chkbox.pl

```perl
#!/usr/bin/perl

require "formparser.lib"; &parseform;

print "Content-type:text/html\n\n<html>";
print "<b>Favorite Destinations Selected:</b><br/>";
foreach $key (keys %formdata)
{
    print "<li>$formdata{$key}";
}
print "</html>";
```

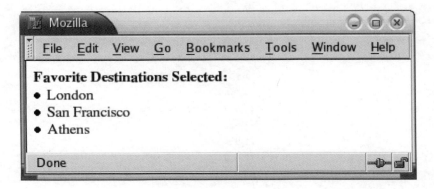

Radio buttons

Radio button inputs are named after the type of real buttons used on old radios that allowed selection of a pre-set station.

Pushing one button de-selected the previous selection, so only one station could be selected at any given time.

In HTML, radio button inputs work in just the same way – allowing only one input to be selected at any given time.

Radio buttons are grouped together by setting their "name" attribute to a common name. That group will then only allow a single button within the group to ever be selected.

Each of the radio buttons in a group have individual values assigned to their "value" attributes that makes them unique.

When a form is submitted, it is the **name=value** pair of the selected radio button in the group that is sent to the server.

The following example illustrates a HTML document containing a form with two groups of radio buttons:

radio.html

Always use meaningful names for the radio button groups.

```html
<html>
<head> <title>Radio Button Groups</title> </head>

<body>
<form method="POST"
      action="http://localhost/cgi-bin/radio.pl">
<b>Select a color: </b>
<input type="radio" name="Color" value="Red"/> Red
<input type="radio" name="Color" value="Green"/> Green
<input type="radio" name="Color" value="Blue"/> Blue
<hr/>
<b>Select a number: </b>
<input type="radio" name="Number" value="One"/> One
<input type="radio" name="Number" value="Two"/> Two
<input type="radio" name="Number" value="Three"/> Three
<hr/>
<input type="submit" value="Submit Selections"/>
</form>
</body>
</html>
```

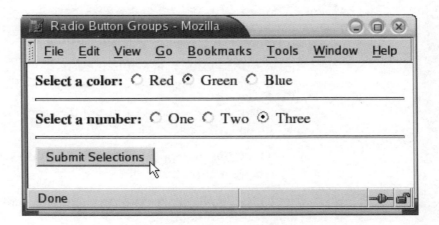

The submitted **name=value** pairs are processed by the form parser and each component is displayed by the HTML output.

radio.pl

```perl
#!/usr/bin/perl

require "formparser.lib"; &parseform;

print "Content-type: text/html\n\n<html>";
print "<h3>Radio Button Selections:</h3>";
foreach $key (keys %formdata)
{
    print "<li>$key selected is $formdata{$key}";
}
print "</html>";
```

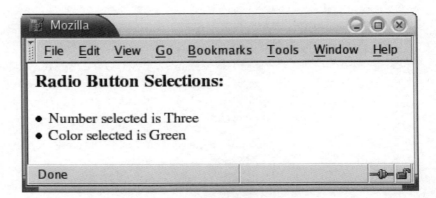

Option menus

The option menus enclosed by the HTML "select" tags allow the user to choose an item from a menu list.

A **name=value** pair sent to the server from an option menu is drawn from separate HTML tags.

The **name** component is that of the "name" attribute specified in the HTML "select" tag.

The **value** component is the "value" of the option that is selected when the form is submitted.

This example creates two option menus with name components of "day" and "month":

menu.html

Omit the size attributes from the "select" tags to have the options display "drop-down" menus.

```html
<html>
<head> <title>Option Menus</title> </head>

<body>
<form method = "POST"
    action = "http://localhost/cgi-bin/menu.pl">
<b>Select A Date: </b> <br/>
<select name = "month" size = "5">
<option value = "January">Jan</option>
<option value = "February">Feb</option>
<option value = "March">Mar</option>
<option value = "April">Apr</option>
<option value = "May">May</option>
</select>

<select name = "day" size = "5">
<option value = "18th">18</option>
<option value = "19th">19</option>
<option value = "20th">20</option>
<option value = "21st">21</option>
<option value = "22nd">22</option>
</select>

<input type = "submit" value = "Submit Date"/>
</form>
</body>
</html>
```

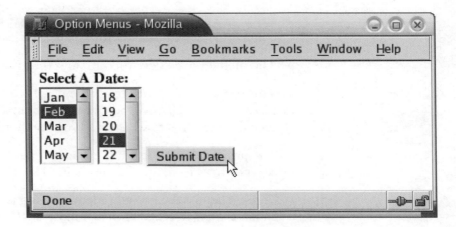

The **name=value** pairs that are submitted by the form are processed by form parser in the usual way.

Each value can be addressed in the "%formdata" hash using the name assigned to the select tag's "name" attribute.

The values are then displayed in the HTML output.

menu.pl

```perl
#!/usr/bin/perl

require "formparser.lib"; &parseform;

print "Content-type:text/html\n\n<html>";
print "<b>Selected Date: </b>";
print "$formdata{'month'} $formdata{'day'}";
print "</html>";
```

Notice that the actual values are verbose versions of the menu items.

All inputs (text, textarea, checkbox, radio and option menus) provide a means for the user to create a name/value pair.

Browser redirection

PERL can be used to redirect a web browser to a HTML page containing content specifically written for just that browser.

The method to achieve this employs the "Location:" header.

For more about "Content-type:" and "MIME" header types see page 14.

This header is used in place of the usual "Content-type:" header that specifies the MIME type. The "Location:" header instead specifies the URL to which the browser should be redirected.

The print statement for the "Location:" header must still end with two newlines to signify that it is a header.

In this example the browser identity string is assigned to a scalar which is then searched to match individual browsers.

The browser will load a page containing content appropriate for either Internet Explorer, Mozilla/Netscape or other browsers.

jump.pl

```
#!C:\Perl\bin\perl

$browser = $ENV{'HTTP_USER_AGENT'};
$target;

if( $browser =~ m/MSIE/i )
{ $target = "http://localhost/ie_page.html" }
elsif( $browser =~ m/Mozilla/i )
{ $target = "http://localhost/moz_page.html" }
else
{ $target = "http://localhost/default.html" }

print "Location: $target\n\n"; exit();
```

For more about matching string patterns see page 102.

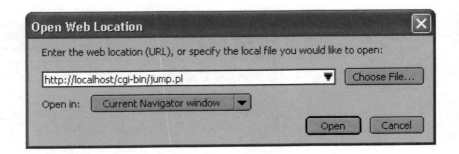

If the web browser is Internet Explorer this page will load:

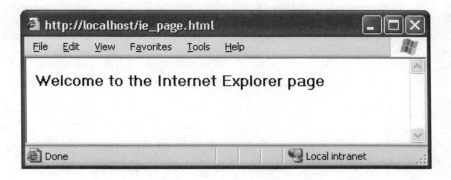

If the web browser is Mozilla or Netscape this page will load:

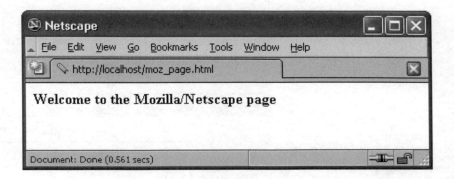

Other browsers will load this default page:

Here the Opera web browser uses its own identity but it can optionally be set to identify itself like Netscape Navigator or Microsoft Internet Explorer.

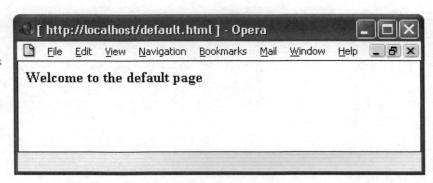

Mail response

A PERL script can send an automatic response by email if the server has an email program available.

Mostly, Unix-based web servers have a program called "sendmail" for this purpose, although its directory location can vary.

Accessing the "sendmail" program from a PERL script is similar to the way that text files are read and written.

The program must first be opened and a file handle label given. A "|" pipe character should immediately precede the "sendmail" location to indicate that it is a program.

Once opened, the "print" function can write the email data. The "close" function must finally close the text stream.

The example illustrates a script located on a Unix server with the PERL interpreter in the "/usr/bin" directory and the "sendmail" program in the "/usr/lib" directory.

After the email data is sent to "sendmail" the script will write a HTML message for the user.

This HTML form submits data to the PERL script from a text input named "adr" and from a text area named "msg".

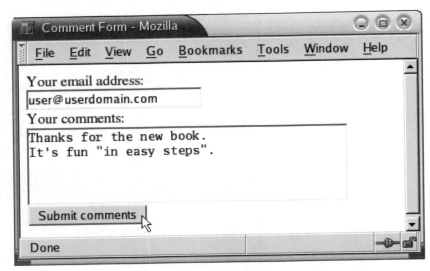

reply.pl

The " -t" switch instructs the "sendmail" program to look for incoming data for "To:", "From:" and "Subject:" message lines.

Always escape special script characters – like the "@" in an email address.

```perl
#!/usr/bin/perl
require "formparser.lib"; &parseform;
$adr = $formdata{'adr'};
$msg = $formdata{'msg'};

open(REPLY, "|/usr/lib/sendmail -t");
print REPLY "To: $adr \n";
print REPLY "From: sender\@serverdomain.com \n";
print REPLY "Subject: Your Comments \n";
print REPLY "This information was submitted:\n";
print REPLY "$msg Your comments are appreciated.";
close REPLY;

print "Content-type:text/html\n\n <html>";
print "<b>Thanks for your input!</b> <br/>";
if ($adr && $msg)
{ print "You should get an autoresponse soon." }
print "<br/>Please click back. </html>";
```

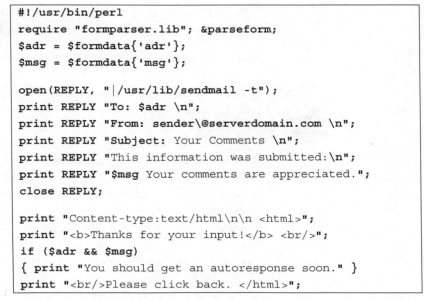

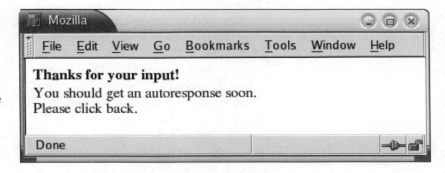

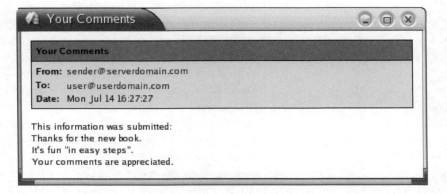

Survey application

The code below creates a HTML document consisting of a single survey form that can be submitted to a PERL script.

This form contains an example of each type of form input.

poll.html

```html
<html><head><title>WWW Survey</title></head>
<body bgcolor="black">
<form method="POST"
    action="http://localhost/cgi-bin/poll.pl">
<table border="1" bgcolor="white" width="100%">
<tr><td>  <b>Please select your browser:</b> <br>
<input type="radio" name="browser" value="Internet
Explorer"/>  Internet Explorer<br/>
<input type="radio" name="browser" value="Netscape"/>
Netscape<br/>
<input type="radio" name="browser" value="Mozilla"/>
Mozilla<br/>
<input type="radio" name="browser" value="Opera"/>
Opera<br/>
<input type="radio" name="browser" value="a minor
browser"/>  Other<br/>
</td></tr><tr><td><b>Where do you access the web ?</b>
<br/><input type="checkbox" name="home" value="at home"/>
At home<br/>
<input type="checkbox" name="work" value="at work"/>
At the office<br/>
<input type="checkbox" name="move" value="on the move"/>
While travelling<br/>
</td></tr><tr><td>    <b>On which platform ?</b>
<select name="platform">
<option value="Windows" selected> Windows </option>
<option value="Unix/Linux"> Unix/Linux </option>
<option value="Minor platform"> Other</option> </select>
</td></tr><tr><td><b>How could the web be improved ?</b>
<textarea rows="3" cols="28" name="idea"></textarea>
</td></tr><tr><td>
<b>Please enter your e-mail address:</b>
<input type="text" size="32" name="user"/>
</td></tr><tr><td>
<input type="submit" value="Click Here To Submit Form"/>
</td></tr></table> </form> </body> </html>
```

Checks could be added to see that all form fields are "required" so that the user cannot submit a partially completed form.

The survey form is shown above with selected user entries.

When the user pushes the submit button, all the form data is sent to the script detailed on the next page.

The form parser separates all the **name=value** pairs so that the script can use their values to write a HTML response page.

Individual tests are made to see if the value exists before writing a descriptive line of text about that entry.

poll.pl

```perl
#!/usr/bin/perl
require "formparser.lib"; &parseform;

print "Content-type:text/html\n\n <html>";
print "<title>Survey Data Received</title>";
print "The following information was received:<p>";
if($formdata{'user'})
{ print "<li>From: $formdata{'user'}" }
if($formdata{'browser'})
{ print "<li>Browser in use is $formdata{'browser'}" }
if($formdata{'home'})
{ print "<li>Web access is available $formdata{'home'}" }
if($formdata{'work'})
{ print "<li>Web access is available $formdata{'work'}" }
if($formdata{'move'})
{ print "<li>Web access is available $formdata{'move'}" }
if($formdata{'platform'})
{ print "<li>Platform used is $formdata{'platform'}" }
if($formdata{'idea'})
{ print "<li>Suggested improvement:<p>$formdata{'idea'}"}
print "<p>Thank you for participating.</html>";
```

Remember to thank users for taking part in this kind of survey.

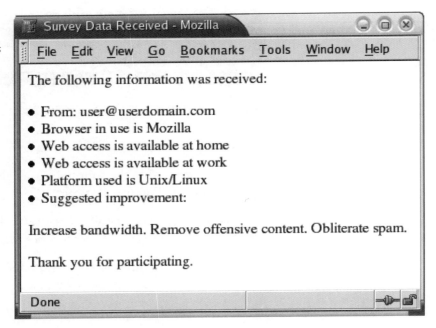

Upload and run scripts

This chapter demonstrates how to upload PERL scripts to a web server, so that they will perform correctly. The use of third-party scripts is explained and some addresses are given where PERL resources can be obtained for free.

Covers

Chapter Fifteen

FTP upload

Running PERL scripts on the Internet normally requires that the files are uploaded to an Internet Service Provider (ISP). The ISP will advise where the scripts must be located on their server, and of any restrictions that they may impose.

It is most convenient to upload files by File Transfer Protocol (FTP) using a FTP Client program. Most ISP servers run a Unix/Linux operating system, but using a FTP Client means that no knowledge of Unix is needed.

Windows users can use Internet Explorer to simply drag 'n' drop script files into the appropriate server directory via FTP.

Some ISPs do not allow PERL scripts – but it's easy to change to another ISP.

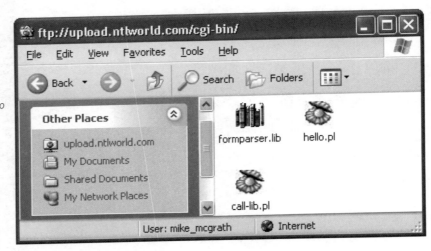

The PERL script location directory may often be the **cgi-bin** directory on the ISP server – in the same way that the examples in this book have been using Apache's **cgi-bin** directory.

It is important to know the location of the PERL interpreter on the ISP server as the "she-bang" line in each PERL script needs to be amended accordingly, before it is uploaded. The "she-bang" line must correctly state the server location of PERL if the script is to run properly from the sever.

To avoid possible problems when loaded on the server, the FTP Client options should always be set to upload scripts as ASCII or text files – not as binary files.

Setting permissions

When PERL script files have been uploaded to the ISP's server, their file permissions need to be set to restrict how the files may be used.

Linux users can set the desired permissions using the **chmod** command. Windows users can set the permissions with Internet Explorer. Right-click on the icon of an uploaded script file, then select "properties" from the context menu. Check the appropriate boxes to set the file permissions.

Owners will always want full permissions but other groups should be denied the permission to write to the files. Library files are not executable, so do not need that permission.

The permissions illustrated in the screenshot below are typical – a numeric value of 755.

The numeric value for permissions are an addition for each group where read=4, write=2 and executable=1. Normally set files and directories to 755 and library files to 644.

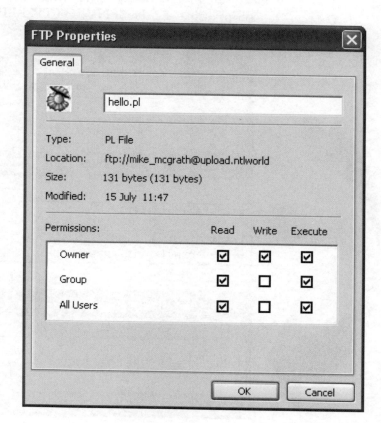

Using the referer

The environment variable **$ENV{'HTTP_REFERER'}** contains the URL of the web page last visited before the PERL script ran.

If the script is run from a HTML document containing a link, then the **$ENV{'HTTP_REFERER'}** variable is set with the URL of the page that contains the link.

This can be useful to gauge where traffic to a website is originating, although it is not wholly accurate, as the variable may have been set in a different manner.

Notice that the spelling of the variable name does not have four "Rs" so is not "HTTP_REFERRER".

For instance, when a script is run by typing its address into the browser's address bar, the **$ENV{'HTTP_REFERER'}** is set with whatever page was last visited by the browser. This happens irrespective of whether that page contains a link to the PERL script.

This example shows a HTML page containing a link to a PERL script displaying the **$ENV{'HTTP_REFERER'}** variable.

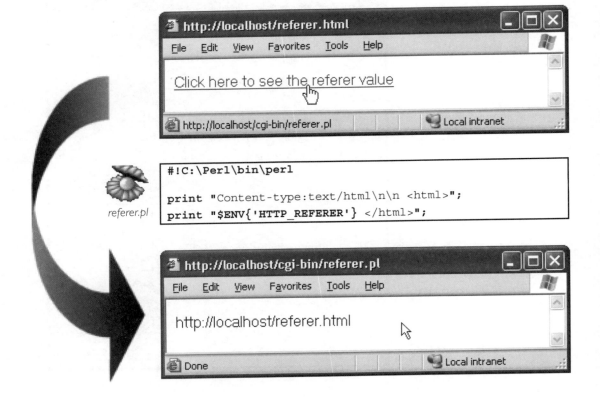

referer.pl

```
#!C:\Perl\bin\perl

print "Content-type:text/html\n\n <html>";
print "$ENV{'HTTP_REFERER'} </html>";
```

Restricted running

The example on the facing page demonstrates that the **$ENV{'HTTP_REFERER'}** variable will be set to the URL of the page containing a link to a PERL script. To ensure that PERL scripts are only run from pages on the same server, this variable can be tested.

The example below checks that the link is contained in a page on the "localhost" server, before permitting the script to run, or will display an alternate message:

local.pl

```
#!C:\Perl\bin\perl

$start = $ENV{'HTTP_REFERER'};
$this_server = "http://localhost/";

print "Content-type:text/html\n\n <html>";
if( $start =~ m/$this_server/i )
{ print "<b>OK: </b>Script accessed from this server." }
else
{ print "<b>Unauthorized Access: </b><br>";
  print "Script cannot run from that location!" }
print "</html>";
```

This top example output was run from the "localhost" domain. The bottom example output was run from another domain.

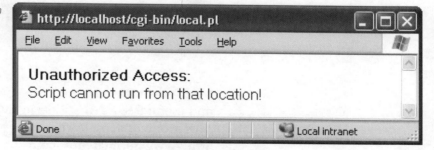

Ready-made scripts and libraries

Lots of ready-made PERL scripts are freely available on the Internet. It is often worthwhile checking to see if a script already exists that can be tailored to meet your needs.

The top three sources recommended by this book to search for ready-made PERL scripts are listed below:

1

The most comprehensive website for PERL with hundreds of scripts, articles and masses of related information at **http://www.cgi-resources.com**.

2

A wealth of scripts in a wide variety of scripting languages including PERL scripts. The lists are broken down into categories that make it easy to find what you need at **http://www.scriptsearch.com**.

3

Matt Wright provides one of the most popular websites to find useful free PERL scripts in "Matt's Script Archive". This is often referred to as simply "MSA" and is located at **http://www.scriptarchive.com**.

Configuring ready-made scripts

When a suitable ready-made script has been located, it will be necessary to configure it to suit its new purpose.

Usually, the author will have provided instructions in the source code to help determine what needs to be changed.

Sometimes the author will have placed all the configurable components in a separate configuration file.

It is good practice to make a back-up copy of the script and all files provided with the script. This provides a quick and easy way to review the original code, if needed.

The first step in configuration is to read the author's notes.

If the script source code contains a copyright notice, any restrictions that may have been placed on how the script may be used, should be observed.

Ensure that the "she-bang" line is set to the location of the PERL interpreter on the server that will run the script.

Similarly, change the path addresses of files and directories to suit the server that will be running the script.

Amend any variable values within the script so that they are appropriate to its new purpose.

The output HTML code will normally need to be changed to suit the new use of the script. Edit the source code to create the appropriate HTML output.

Using the information and examples contained in this book, the script may be further customized, until it completely fulfils the precise requirements of its new role.

As with all scripts, it should be tested thoroughly in as many ways as possible, before it is uploaded to the server.

The author may like to learn of any useful additions or amendments that have been made to the original script.

It is always courteous to send an email to the author to say a "Thank You" for providing a free script resource.

More PERL resources

This book will, hopefully, have provided you with a great introduction to the use of PERL in server-side scripts and may have whetted your appetite to find out even more.

The first place to look is the comprehensive PERL documentation that accompanies the PERL interpreter in the download package from Active State.

The documentation includes much more detail on PERL for use in CGI and other applications.

www.perl.com

To learn of the latest PERL developments, and much more, the PERL website is essential viewing.

In addition to PERL news, all versions of the PERL interpreter are available from here in both source code and binary version for a variety of operating systems.

PERL documentation can also be downloaded from this site.

There is a very useful Frequently Asked Questions (FAQ) section and a searchable Reference section that can prove immensely helpful when developing PERL skills.

Feature articles on PERL provide interesting reading too, and the site has links to many PERL tutorials and training courses.

Visitors can subscribe to "The Perl Journal" quarterly magazine to keep regularly posted about new PERL events.

Details of forthcoming PERL conferences are posted and there is a selection of programming tools for download.

Lastly, the site provides a link to the Comprehensive Perl Archive Network (CPAN) which is mirrored at over 100 sites. This aims to provide all the PERL material you will ever need and contains literally hundreds of megabytes of data.

This rich supply of information provides many avenues to explore if you wish to build upon the knowledge you have gained from "PERL in easy steps" – happy scripting!

Index